Driftwood

Dorothy Whipple

BIBLIOLIFE

DRIFTWOOD

By DOROTHY WHIPPLE

PRIVATELY PRINTED
AT THE RIVERSIDE PRESS
1916

DEDICATED TO MY FATHER

CONTENTS

CONTENTS

CONTENTS

CONTENTS

CONTENTS

CONTENTS

CONTENTS

CONTENTS

DRIFTWOOD

DRIFTWOOD

It was night,
A night that God had planned before the world
    began.
The moon glimmered in a gold surprise
Over a wine-spilled sea. A creature of to-day
In all the words he knows could not express
What the moon saw, and the moon will not speak
    of this night.
There was one soul on the shore beside the wave-
    crested sea;
I think it was mine own, but the wind could not
    tell me;
Or perhaps it was that I could not understand
    that night.
Far out on the swaying murmurous moontide,
I saw mermaids frolicking with the foam in
    ecstatic gracefulness:
Their hair glinted in the velvet moonlight
And spread a golden vein into the wine luster of
    the sea.
There were fairies catching the star-pierced
    spray

DRIFTWOOD

Of the breaking waves.
I heard a child's voice, I think she woke from her
      sleep
And knew that this night was not like others.
Children always know such things:
It is because they have come so lately from God
Who holds the silver cords of the plasmatic
      world.
There was no voice in me.
The sea spoke, but I could not answer it,
Or understand the words it trampled out.
Then morning came out of the sea.
One of the mermaids gleaned the exquisite pink
Of the conch-shell and threw it to the skies;
My soul saluted the dawn:
The morning star shivered and glided
Behind the curtain of a pearl mist.
Then I awoke, and as one in a dream
Walked forth from under the wings of that
      night
Which was left over in the oil of centuries.
There was driftwood on the beach;
There was the echo of a child's laugh in a shell;
And there were fairies held prisoners
Under the foam-bubbles on the silvered sand.

DRIFTWOOD

There must be a beautiful garden under the
      green sea,
Because I found blossoms of spring and summer
      flowers
Of all shades, and the fragrant flowers
That come in the honeyed autumnal days.
My soul will never forget that night
And the things it found in the morning
On the lovely long beach.
It talks about those things to me in strange
      echoes now.
I have saved some of the driftwood;
Some day I will burn it all, see
The blue flame, and hear the echo
Of the murmurous sea-thunder.

IN THE NET

IN THE NET

A LONE fisherman
Out on the great expanse of the lapis-lazuli sea.
With the millions of glinting gold sunbeams
That ride the ecstatic wavelets,
His white boat rises and falls on the water
Like a recurrent thought, —
Now lost in the vast blueness, now dazzlingly
        visible,
Like a speck of foam.

There is something flying through the radiance
        of the morning air;
It is not a gull.
The gulls gaze on it with lazy surprise;
It has wings and it is my soul.
It must reach the lone fisherman before his net
        is drawn.
Now he is reaching over the side of the white
        foam boat,
And it tips to meet the blue
Till the dull brown floor and sides are visible,
With the ropes and pails and shining fish-scales.

IN THE NET

And the lone fisherman is pulling his heavy net
  over the side.
There is a glinting mass of animation through
  the meshes of the net,
And the slippery sound of captured fish
As they lash their bodies about
Swimming in the foreign air.
There are many fish in the net, but there is more
  beside
From the wonderful ocean-green depths beyond
  the silence of the sea song.
There is a conch-shell with elusive pink tints:
One would follow that shade to the heart were
  it possible.
The wind is singing beautifully of the mysteries
  of the sky,
And the sunbeams are playing on the harp of the
  air.
In the conch-shells are the echoes of songs —
Beauteous strains vaguely inexpressible.
There are rainbow bubbles all about.
The occasional flip of a fish breaks one now and
  then,
And the rainbow streams lavishly over his shining
  scales.

IN THE NET

Then another foam-bubble appears.
And the rainbow flows together and becomes a
      drop of water.
It looks like a beautiful tear from the depths of
      despair,
Where it is purple and dark with suffering.
Tears are like snowdrops
Bleeding out of the ground.
A sea-anemone was caught in the net.
It had a lost dream in its chalice.
Some one out at sea forgot a dream.
It fell into the ocean and lay
In the anemone's beautiful cup.
There was a flash of gold amid the silvered fish-
      scales.
The meshes of the net were lying on it heavily,
And a starfish clung to one end.
Could it be that the fisherman had caught the
      crescent moon?
It was its reflection.
There was a night when the sea was idly calm
And the moon threw its reflection down.
The moon's reflection is its love;
And a beautiful pink starfish
Caught the crescent moon's love and held it fast.

IN THE NET

The fisherman caught them both.
The silent tide is creeping in;
The fisherman must get home.
He empties all but the fish into the dizzy sea
      again.
There is only an occasional flash and flicker of
      sunbright scales;
Most of the fish are dry and sticky.
My soul saw all that came up from the sea's
      depth
In the fisherman's coarse brown net.
It has left the boat now,
And the gulls float in the vast blueness,
And they see my soul passing again.
It is coming to me and I shall know all.

A PEARL — A KISS

A STAR fell into the depths of the sea —
A star of golden mystery;
And the rainbow flight of the ocean spray
Mingled and made it a pearl where it lay.

A thought fell into the depths of a heart,
And felt its quivering pulses start;
The rainbow dreams that arise from our bliss
Touched it — and it became a kiss.

UNANSWERED

WHY is it wrong to long for death?
She stands gazing at the sun-bright water
Asking the breeze,
Asking the trees,
Why is it wrong to long for death?

The waters are beating against the sand;
With the same insistent beat, pain throbbed
        'gainst her heart
Until it saw the life-blood oozing start,
Until it left her hopeless on the strand.

There is no need to flaunt her suffering —
I think that words would fail. Let those who
        know
Life, those who understood it long ago,
Realize that sacred silence which bespeaketh all.

Why is it wrong to long for death?
She stands gazing at the deep gray waters,
Asking the wind,
Asking her mind,
Why is it wrong to long for death?

LONGING

THERE is a longing in my soul
For rainbow things
Far, far away.
There is a rustle on the breeze
Of fairy wings
Far, far away.

Gently my life-pulse beats into the night;
Slowly my sleep-soul rises to the light;
Gold of the moonbeams shimmering o'er the lea,
Heart of my heart, I am calling thee.

There is a longing in my soul
For mystic things
Far, far away.
There is a distant echoing voice
That murmuring sings
Far, far away.
My love is throbbing like the evening star,
Caught in the purple haze of night afar;
Foam-crested waves are breaking near the sea;
Heart of my heart, I am calling thee.

GOOD-NIGHT

GOOD-NIGHT, dear one, good-night.
The lily hath let her petals white
Close to the murmur of the night,
Lulled by a faint star-distant beam,
The spirit of a beautiful dream.
Good-night, dear one, good-night.

Good-night, dear one, good-night.
The breeze is whispering to the moon,
The harp of night is all in tune,
And over the sea where the mermaids glide
A path of gold sways with the tide.
Good-night, dear one, good-night.

Good-night, dear one, good-night.
The moon is drawing the sighing sea;
My love, thy heart is drawing me,
And the flowers droop in the ambient air
To breathe on the silver moonbeams there.
Good-night, dear one, good-night.

Good-night, dear one, good-night.
The promise-star in the deep blue sky

GOOD–NIGHT

Hath gleamed — we shall meet again,
    thou and I,
And I shall know thy smile of light
In the lovely land of a fond good-night.
Good-night, dear one, good-night.

SLEEP

BEAUTIFUL over the sunlit sea,
Dreamy over the hyacinth lea,
Drowsy tops of the swaying tree —
Sleep — O sleep, thou art come to me.

Far in a land of dream-desires,
Of rainbow bubbles and fairy spires,
Where lilies are growing in clouds of white,
And breathing fragrance to the stars' light;

Deep in the realm of the evening star,
Where translucent spirits of mystery are;
Sleep, thou hast taken me far away
From the life I live in the sparkling day.

Beautiful over the morning sea,
Lovely the jasamine skies to me;
The crocus dawn is warm with light
From the shimmering moonbeams of the night.

DREAMS ARE BEST

IT is so fair to dream life,
Dream till reality
Becomes a mist that trembles
Over a seething sea;
To lay down the cross we're bearing,
Just for a little while,
And after the tears of suffering
Feel the warm sun of a smile.

It is so fair to dream love,
Nor put it to life's acid test;
Its anguish consumes the heart so.
Oh, dreams are the very best.

THE SICKLE THAT REAPS THE STARS

Out of the tow'ring cave of night
Where the dreams of mortals are,
A radiant youth of spirit light
Came forth and journeyed afar.

Gold as the rays of the setting sun,
Shone the moon-sickle in his hand,
To reap the trembling evening stars
That sparkle like silver sand.

Gladly he reaped in the purple field,
Gathering star by star;
The gold moon-sickle grew fainter — till
'Twas lost in the distance far.

MY SOUL

My soul is wandering far away
Into the crocus of waning day,
Into the distant amethyst
Of the ever-drooping, fading mist.

I watch it shimmering o'er the sea
Like a trembling breath of eternity;
I see it on a sunbeam far
Melt into the evening star.

It glimmers like a firefly
Into the purple of the sky.
The moaning sea to the foam-white beach
Answers its echo's utmost reach.

And my soul is palpitating still
With the pulse of the star over the hill.
Where will it be when that golden star
Shall fade in the light of the morning far?

FATE

FATE with a trembling hand wrote this —
A line of suffering, a line of bliss,
And life glides on in a mist of tears
Or a rainbow of hope that hides our fears.
But the lines that were written by fate shall be
Realized for all eternity.

JUST FOR TO-NIGHT

Just for to-night, dear, come unto me;
Forget all the pains and sorrows that be;
Just for to-night, dear, take thou my hand —
Let us live life as our two hearts had planned.

Just for to-night, dear, take me and say
You love me and you will love me alway;
Just for to-night, dear, kiss me again,
The kiss that I dreamed would never be pain..

A RHAPSODY

Blue sky, green fields and fleecy clouds of
  white!
Their strange shaped shadows glide like dreams
  of night
Over the silent fields of swaying grain,
Great visions of the spirit of the plain.
Under the leafy trees in cool deep glades
Soft, golden sunlight slowly gleams and fades.
White phantom visions flit before the eyes
And vanish in the distance of the skies.
Rippling, splashing water on the golden sand,
A gently stirring sound, — perhaps Titania's
  band.
And all the dryads of the woodland trees
In rainbow circles flit upon the breeze.
Dryads robed in purple like the iris light,
Opalescent fairies, spirits of dusky night.
Fairies, fairies, fairies soaring to the skies,
Let us wait a little longer till the moon shall rise.
Then the rainbow fairies, combing all the light,
Shall shimmer through the darkness into stars of
  night.

IMMORTAL HOURS

Hours long I stop and listen
To the singing harp of time;
And I hear soft, distant echoes
Harking from another clime.

Echoes of the past are trembling
In music through the halls of life;
Angel hands that bear loved memories
Charm away all sordid strife.

As the primrose sky of evening
Fades into the purple night,
So those memories, softly blending,
Mingle in my heart's delight.

Memories of such perfect hours
Pass like moonbeams o'er the sea;
Hours of reading and communing,
Soul to soul, upon the lea.

Hours that e'er shall be immortal,
Ensouled in rainbow memories;

IMMORTAL HOURS

Life may take our fond desires,
Turn our joys to tragedies.

But, like petals of a flower,
Velvet soft and misty light,
Memories of such bliss shall linger
Breathing fragrance through death's night.

BEYOND

ALWAYS a mystic distance luring us on through
life;
Always a fear immortal after the storm of strife;
Always a vision rising over accomplishment's
peak;
Always intangible glories for which we may ever
seek.

And watch, vanishing, vanishing, like gulls over
the sea;
And our eyes dwell on that distance, fancying
what might be.
And then comes the end of life, and still the great
to be,
Something forever beyond our grasp, the last is
eternity.

HATE

WHEN the first flush of rosy light
Gleamed through the curtain of the night,
And all the flowers of the morn
Gazed in the mirror of the dawn,

A gentle breeze came o'er the lea,
Over the purple jasmine sea,
Searching a flower to love and woo,
As the light breeze of morning joys to do.

A lily trembled and opened her heart,
Pure as the golden sunbeam-dart;
The wandering breeze caressed her all day
Till evening came on her starry way.

And the lily closed her petals white
To dream of the breeze and day's delight;
Under the mystic stars she lay,
Like a pure thought when the heart would pray.

And in this world where life is so strange
All are flower-weak and all things change;

HATE

Love in a night is turned to hate;
We would enter heaven, but find it too late.

The evening breeze and the lily white
Changed in the span of a mortal night:
She heard him roar and sigh and groan
And shriek in a moaning undertone.

A wind of hate is a wind that kills,
And breaks the substance of our wills.
Next morning the blossom had drooped her
      head, —
A flower was found in the garden, dead.

THOU

Star distant all my hopes and all my fears,
Silent as death the life-blood of my heart
Flows in a purple stream. Pain cannot start
The wild sad thrill it used in other years,
Nay, nor the bitter bleeding, blinding tears.
Oh joy, a hazy memory thou art,
Tinged faintly with gleams that could once
   impart
Such raptures! Dreamy aurora enspheres
My being in a golden mesh of light.
Pain, longing, sorrow, and a dear delight
Are mingled like the breath of a pearl mist,
Faintly they touch the senseless cheek, insist,
Like beating rain, till, my beloved, pain
Withdraws her hand and thou art near again.

PENELOPE'S WEB

DEAREST, I cannot say good-bye to thee.
The pallid moon may urge the stars to shine,
But, O beloved, lay thy hand on mine,
And all the trembling flame of love leaps free,
Consumes my throbbing heart, and thus leaves
      me
Helpless in thy sight. I lift my eyes to thine
And see the image of a life divine,
Lived close to God in beauty still to be.
Ah no, I cannot say good-bye, dear heart.
The words are vain, and yet I love to part,
For all the sweetness of farewell — I say,
Good-bye, and with the first breath of to-day
Undo those silver words, as she who spun
All day till night and then unravelled all she'd
      done.

THE CALL

THE sunbeams are glimmering through the trees,
The flowers sway in the evening breeze.
Why do you hasten on, little brook?
Laughing waters, why leave this nook
Where the sand is soft and gold
And the wild-rose petals fold?
Why hasten on to the hungry sea?
Is this happiness not enough for thee,
With all this beauteous solitude,
The water-lily diamond-dewed?
The sea is calling for the brook
For the echoes of its quiet nook,
Rippling, laughing brook so free
Why be lost in that boundless sea?

THEIR SON

THE yellow sunlight flickered through the trees;
Slowly the fluttering leaves, gold and red,
Fell through the silent air from overhead
Upon the twilight of two lives. The evening
      breeze
Mingled its whispers with the drone of bees.
Beyond their tear-dimmed vision, far ahead,
Lay purple hills with misty light o'erspread;
Their vision rested upon each of these.
Silent they stood, those two, gazing far away
At that lone figure going out to meet the day
Beyond the hills, leaving the autumn leaves to
      fall,
Like the hopes of their hearts and taking all.
All but a dream of what had ceased to be,
Tinged with a longing, aching misery.

HYPNOS

FAIR HYPNOS of the peaceful, dreamy brows,
Who weary mortals mystic rest allows,
Come to me now and lay thy cool, soft hand
Over my weary eyes. Unloose each band
Of pain's relentless woe that all the day
Like coiling serpents strangles peace away.
As falls the sunlight on the purple hills,
So falls thy comfort on the wayward wills
Of men. O'er seething seas a dream of night
Is melting into soft radiant light.
The evening star will gently draw it soon,
Out of the shimmering bosom of the moon,
And I shall dream of fountains in the sun,
Of summer sunsets when the day is done,
Of cloud-flecked skies whose shadows on the
   grass
Glide by the golden sunbeams and pass
On to the hills, and then far, far away
To wait the dawn of coming day.

TEARS AND DEWDROPS

THE evening breeze wafts o'er the sea,
Breathing its fragrance and sweetness to me,
And it faints in the flush of the sunset sky
While the languorous gulls are soaring by.

The breath of my pain is drifting too
Somewhere afar in God's heaven of blue.
The morning wind is fresh and clear
It misses a dewdrop and finds a tear.

MORNING

INTO the mists of sunshine,
Into the violet sky,
The morning star is waning
And our dreams are floating by.

Out of the mists of morning,
Out of the rainbow dew,
The radiant day is dawning
And morn is coming anew.

Out of the dreams and visions,
Out of the purple night,
The spirit of mortal is stirring
And reveling in the light.

PROMISE

THE lilies are lulled to sleep by the wind,
And the glamorous world is left behind
As the golden sheen of meteor light,
When a star falls into the unknown night.

The lilies are breathing soft and low,
And their perfume sleeps in the breezes that blow,
And over the purple hills far away
God is pouring life into the day.

With promise of undreamed things to be,
Moments of pain and ecstasy,
We never know till the day is o'er
The mystery God hath planned before.

THANKS

DEAR FRIEND, you sang for her one perfect
    night,
The halo of thy voice wreathed round her heart
And quivered there till it became a part
Of life to her at best. Her rare delight
Was pictured in her eyes from the soul's insight.
It is not strange that longing tears should start
And tremble in the recess of the heart
On hearing those sweet strains again. To-night
I thought I felt her presence lingering near,
A spirit by thy music bidden, here,
She heard; perhaps not as she heard before,
But with us still and loving even more.
How vain a word of thanks must seem to thee;
Yet thou knowest how deep our thanks must be.

LIFE'S FACETS

'T is a world of childish bliss,
Of care-free days and happiness:
What could fairer be than this?
　　When hearts are young.

'T is a world of dawning dreams,
With its rainbow pain-tinged gleams,
And love's tender trembling beams
　　Of our youth.

'T is a world of love and light,
Thrilling heart-throbs of delight;
Of a new and deep insight
　　Into life.

'T is a world of tender pain,
When we feel all strife is vain;
There's a face we'll see again
　　Never more.

'T is a world of sacrifice
In which perfect pardon lies,

LIFE'S FACETS

With a glimpse of Paradise
   Far away.

'T is a world of resignation,
Of long hours of contemplation,
With a dawn of God's relation
   After life.

'T is a world beyond our sight,
Beyond death's grief-darkened night;
And we wait on God for light
   In this world.

'T is a world of blinding grief,
When the heart knows no relief;
Only prayer and firm belief
   Shall avail.

A GOLD RING

Just a gold ring — the moon's mysterious light
Hath played with in the forest heart some night
And made a gold ring: — it has no ending,
Nor beginning, just a mystic blending.

Just a gold ring — hovering round I see
The misty dream of all life held for me
The day, 't was not so very long ago,
It clasped my finger. God, I loved it so!

That dear gold ring — there is a vision now
Of days that passed like music faint and low;
I never knew but faintly guessed
They were too subtly sublime to bear life's test.

CRUSHED BAY

I CRUSHED some bay-leaves with a thoughtless
      hand;
So is it that pain crushes — you understand;
And yet we love the fragrance of crushed bay
And love the visions of a by-gone day.

MEETING

I MET myself the other day,
As I walked through the sunlit fields
Where the shadows of clouds float slowly by
And the clover her fragrance yields.

I walked through the swaying grasses
That rippled and bent in the breeze;
I listened to lisping leaflets
That rustled in bird-haunted trees.

And there in the scented meadow,
Where daisies and red grass grow,
I met myself in the sunshine
And I spoke to myself soft and low.

I asked myself many a question,
But the answers I'll never tell.
It is so strange to meet one's self —
But you've done it, I know full well.

THE WRONG DREAM

ONCE through a gold-beamed twilight,
Over a murmurous sea,
The dream of some other mortal
Wafted out to me.

I saw in the faint, far distance,
Through a mist of opal light,
Something trembling and quivering
And growing forever more bright.

I dreamed that the moon was shining
Over a purple plain,
And someone was faintly calling,
Calling, calling in vain.

I would the other mortal
Had dreamed that dream last night,
And answered the voice on the purple plain
Under the moon's soft light.

Even the angels of dreamland
Once in an æon or so
Touch to life the wrong vision,
But few of us mortals know.

MY OTHER LIFE

WHEN the fire flame is flickering
And the wind is sighing low,
Visions come and angel voices
Whisper of a long ago.

Strange the vision that arises
Of another life than mine,
Other hopes and other longings:
What was then this life of thine?

Were we both strange different beings
Foreign in each other's eyes?
No, for I have felt thee near me
In these visions that arise.

What a world of whims and fancies!
In the valley of the moon
Long ago I think I wandered
And the height of night was noon.

Far away the star of evening
Glimmered, and I loved to see
All its perfect light a-quiver,
Dear heart, for I knew 't was thee.

THE COBWEBS OF CONVENTION

So let us strive to realize our intention
And sweep away the cobwebs of convention,
Those silver threads of life that hold us here
When all the while we feel our ideal near,
Breathing, a new soul clamoring for birth,
A flower, held by winter in the earth.
Let us stretch forth the trembling arm of hope
And, soaring, feel the hands that used to grope,
Touch a new chord whose echoes vibrant fill
The super-soul and tremble there until
The vision shall be realized. Then shall start
A fresh new life with beauty at its heart.

SOULS

THERE are two souls in me that greet the day —
One here, the other star-distant away,
Over the massive hills of night, where sleep
And all the mysteries of visions keep
Their drowsy vigil. The other soul is near,
Crowned with a fragile wreath of fear,
And all its whiteness lies in silent peace,
Watching the fleet shadows of life increase.

SILENCE

WHAT if for one brief moment my wild heart
Were still, and all the dreams of thee that are
So close to it should drift away afar
Like white mists drawn by breath of dawn apart.

The very pulse within me would be still,
I would be dead, and all my love for thee
A flower more for God's eternity,
A world and a heart in silence at his will.

What if for one strange moment all the world
Were silent still as the depths of night,
Deprived of breath, still as a golden shaft of
        light,
Still as the white rose petals all unfurled.

The busy city would stand still a time,
The brook would cease to flow, the breeze to sigh,
Fair leaves to whisper as it passes by,
All lost in silence of a great sublime.

RADIANT EVENING STAR

THE sun of our life arises
Behind the white mists of time,
In the delicate opal colors
Tinged with our dreams divine.
And the mists of time float onward
Down to death's deep sea,
Till they vanish in mystic distance —
We call it eternity.
For one last perfect moment
The sunset of life is aglow;
Slowly the soft shades mingle
And the winds of Elysium blow.
Ah, bright and radiant evening star,
Thy concentrated light
Is the soul of life's fair sunset
Gathered through death's dark night.

THE LAST TIME

WERE this the last time I could see thee, dear,
Were my dreams gathered like mist clouds o'er
      the sea
In pallid whiteness, floating far from me!
Though all my hopes were echoed in a tear,
Still, dearest one, to feel thy presence near
Even for one brief moment — that would be
Joy, rare enough for all eternity,
And I would then forget all else I fear —
Forget the aching pain of loneliness,
Forget the silent hours when I stand
In anguish, reaching out my trembling hand,
Longing, O dear one, for thy loved caress.
The lily forgets all but the pure gleam
Of tender light from a loved moonbeam.

WHO PASSED?

I WONDER who passed here just after the snow fell.
It's a long, long way from home
In the silence, and I cannot tell
    Who passed.

Perhaps a wanderer seeking light —
It's a lonely place to spend the night;
Perhaps a hunter tracking the deer
And yet there are no other tracks near.
No, it was none of these that passed
And faced the ice and the snowy blast.
The tracks are not deep in the drifted snow;
Perhaps a spirit, but where did it go?
On, on and on through the purple night,
Over fields of flake snow banked so white.
Perhaps I only dreamed I saw tracks, how
Strange and yet, I see them even now.

I wonder who did pass here just after the snow fell.
It's a long, long way from home
In the silence, and I cannot tell
    Who passed.

SUNRISE

THE dusky night on quiet wings upborne
Hath flown far away;
The morning star that ushers in the dawn
Is budding into day.
Far off the first warm petals are unfurled,
And wait but the kiss
Of the dawn sprite, Elysian; dew-impearled,
To blossom into this,
This radiant splendor of the rising sun,
This promise of a star,
This moment of communion with the skies
And regions still afar.

RAIN AND WIND

THERE are secrets in the whisper of the rain.
There is music in a tender, minor strain,
Echoes from the heart that throbs in pain
For all that ne'er will come in life again.
Ah, the whisper of the soft melodious rain.

There are secrets in the moaning of the wind,
Soul visions that our heart hath left behind,
With the music of loved voices, low and kind,
And a memory in the recess of the mind.
Oh, the secrets of the moaning, sighing wind.

ANTITHESIS

THE poem of the evening star
To the song of the purple night;
The blending of dreams and thoughts
With the ecstasy of delight.

The delicate thrill of joy
To the tender music of pain;
The reflected ray of light
In a trembling drop of rain.

The tumult of life and love
To the dream of its quiet hours;
The delicate beauty of life
To its virile and perfect powers.

The poem of a longing heart
To the echo from far away;
The dream of suffering night,
And love is born with the day.

TIME

TIME held her hands together long ago,
And day by day with dreamy eyes watched pass,
Slowly like shimmering stars, life's grains of sand
That fell unseen upon the verdant grass.

But now her lily fingers draw apart;
Still she is standing with dreamy eyes,
And all the golden sand like shafts of light
Slips through and lies in suffered tragedies.

This is the end. And yet she stands there still,
A golden heap of life existent near,
And all around new grains of sand fall through —
But mine is now a heap and sere.

DREAMS AND WAKING

WHAT is a dream?
A breath from the petals of a flower,
A perfect moment of one glad hour,
The rainbow after a summer shower,
The kiss of mysterious night.

What is awakening?
A dreaming sense of what has been,
Of voices heard, loved faces seen;
A butterfly moment poised between
Mystery and reality.

BUBBLES

You say that the heart forgets, dear,
Forgets the joy and the pain;
Stands waiting, an empty bubble,
Till life shall tinge it again.

There are bubbles that float in the air, dear,
Reflecting the sunset shades;
There are bubbles that soar to heaven
In color that swirls and fades.

There are bubbles that fall to earth, dear,
And are lost in a sea of dreams;
There are bubbles that tremble e'er melting
Into pain's deep purple gleams.

The heart does not forget, dear,
Though frail as a bubble it be;
The heart can never forget, dear,
Till utmost eternity.

SOUL OF MY SOUL

SOUL of my soul, — life of my life, —
I come to thee over the hills of chance,
Out of the mists of circumstance;
Peace in my heart from all the strife.

Soul of my soul, — heart of my very heart, —
I heard thy voice throughout the silent night
Long, long ago, and saw thy soul light
And mine own become a part.

Soul of my soul, — breath of my very breath, —
Our lives have drawn together as the night
Melts into the mystery of daylight
We love, and see thus mingling life and death.

CANDLE–LIGHT

In the candle-light of life,
When the sun is set,
Come the shadows of the past
We tried to forget.

Great dark shadows like the clouds
That used to bank the sky,
But always leave the sunshine
When they had passed by.

PLYMOUTH SEAWEED

PLYMOUTH SEAWEED

THERE was a long shore,
And the silver sand sparkled in the moonlight,
And the proud crested waves
Rose and crashed, groveling on the glinting
    sand,
And the white foam scintillated under the silent
    moonbeams
Beneath the sea. — Under the long golden
    smile of the moon
The spirits of the deep played in swaying grace-
    fulness.
There were long-haired mermaids
Who tore the green brown seaweed from the rocks
And flung it to the golden moon-ripples.
There were fishes with huge eyes and little
    mouths
Darting about in the green gold waters —
Old fishes with long fins and sunken gills;
They sat in the shadows
And told all they knew.
They told of the first boat
That came years and years ago to these waters;

PLYMOUTH SEAWEED

How it stayed only a short while and went away
Leaving the pilgrims behind.
The fishes have never seen just such a boat since.
Many other boats have been in the harbor,
Bringing many pilgrims,
But the fishes remember the first one best.
The old fishes remember what the gulls have told
      them.
The gulls float over the land,
And their round, bright eyes see many things;
Then they soar back again,
With long, lazy wings that touch the waters.
That is the way they talk to the folk of the sea
Of all the mysteries of the land each year.
The gulls have told the old fishes of the life there,
Of the struggle for existence,
Of the flight of some,
And of the ones who have stayed there long years,
Of their loves, tragedies, joys and sorrows,
Of their winters and summers.
The old fishes know a great deal,
And they love to tell it
As they glide back and forth in the long caress-
      ing seaweed
That slips by their glistening scaly sides.

PLYMOUTH SEAWEED

And still the graceful long-haired mermaids
Tear the gold green seaweed
And fling it to the smile of the moon.
In the morning a young man
With an echo of the moon's smile on his lips,
And dark brown eyes,
Comes and gathers the seaweed,
His old horse stands on the beach,
Switching his tail at the flies
That the sea breezes do not blow off, —
Switching it perhaps from force of habit.
He is like some of the people the gulls tell about.
They have done strange things for years,
And still do them and their children do them too
       in the same way.

It is a beautiful sun-clear morning,
The wind is fresh and the sky is bright blue;
The man has gathered the seaweed, nor
Does he know of the beautiful mermaids who
       plucked it,
And of the æon-old fishes of the deep.
He is carrying it home now
Along the little sandy road
With dusty grasses and wild roses bordering it;

PLYMOUTH SEAWEED

And then through the fields with daisies and
    clovers,
Just before he reaches his home, —
The little white house with green blinds
Under the shadows of the foothills,
The farmers know that seaweed
Is good for the grass.

CRANBERRIES

THE pitch-pines are gnarled and sturdy;
Glimpses of forget-me-not blue sky
Gleam through the tracery of their needles.
The oaks that grow among them
Are a wonderful purple brown, in the fall
When the nights are dew-cool,
And there is a mysterious white mist in the little
     dells.
The flying fairies are held prisoners in the am-
     bient mist
And you can hear their wings rustling all about.
The sun rises in gold and purple,
And the cranberry bogs are bright almost as
     though
They had caught fire from the coming light;
The slender little vines creep over the white
     sand,
Each leaf purpling to the sunrise.
There is a great gray hawk soaring over the bog,
Marring the fleckless blue of the noon sky;
The streams that cut the bogs in squares
Are full of frogs and little fish

CRANBERRIES

That dart on the yellow sand
And make little slivers of animated shadows.
The water is bright and cool; it ripples so im-
portantly;
It is always trying to leap up the vine-covered
bank,
But it slips gleamingly back again
Until the brook is dammed to flood the bog;
Then it creeps in silver gloatingly through the
vines,
To drown the pests or keep frost away.
No wonder the little brook ripples so import-
antly
Over its motley pebbles and silvered sands.
The cranberry bogs are beautiful in the morn-
ing;
All the fairies that were caught in the haze
Become tears in the morning;
If they do not fall into sad hearts,
They glisten in sparkling happiness
On the cranberry vines, and they are full of color
and light.
Fairies are always beautiful and happy
Whatever form they take.
It will soon be time to pick the hard red berries

CRANBERRIES

And the pickers with their dark skins
And bright fantastic clothes
Look as though they might be some fairy pirates
Searching for a buried treasure.
And the sky smiles a blueness down upon the
Bright pink and flaming red and the Tyrian
      purple
And upon the white barrels
Filled with the luscious crimson of the cran-
      berries.

THE FARM

I

BEHIND the house is the meadow,
And beyond the meadow where clovers grow,
And flaming poppies 'mid daisies like the snow,
Serpenting through the grasses is the silver lake
With sunlight on it and trees that shake
Their leaves on to its surface; they float
Each with a fairy in the petalled boat
Over the golden gleams of shadowed sand
On to the great unknown fairy-land.
Beyond the river is another field.
I never went to it, but the waters say
There are daisies there too, and poppies gay;
That the bluebird floats and alights to see
If his soft breast is clover-red. The bee
Buzzes his drowsy monotone
In that field just as he does in our own.
Beyond the fields and river blue hills rise;
Sometimes it is hard to tell them from the skies.
And white clouds fold upon them, till we see
Visions of cloud-land where hills used to be.

THE FARM

These hills seem always calling to the flowers,
And the spirits of the meadow through the
    sunny hours
Breathe back their answers in the faint per-
    fume
That gently wafts so often to my room —
The one just under the roof where the swallows
    build
And the rain beats when the night is wild.
I love to hear the storm spirits shrieking loud.
The ruler of the storm is fierce and proud;
He lashes all the trees and beats the rain
Until it fairly bounces on the window-pane.
He rides the lightning and holds the thunder,
    till
The deep sound rumbles on from hill to hill.
I love my room with its flowers on the wall
There used to be many — the sun has taken
    nearly all;
They are faded flowers now, pressed and put
    away —
Fragile, but they hold the all of a by-gone
    day.

THE FARM

II

I think we're having doughnuts to-night;
They'll be all sugary and yellow and light;
And an apple-pie, I smelled that too,
And we'll have it on the plate with blue
Houses and trees and meadows where grow
Blue flowers not like the field flowers though.
Then the stars'll come out; I've always thought
That when it was dark the fairies brought
All the good daisies up to the sky,
And then they were stars — so often I
Tried to wait for the morning light,
To see the stars in their earthward flight,
Gliding down to the meadows fair;
They are daisies as soon as they get there.
I never could see them, for I fell asleep
And dreamed that I was trying to peep;
And the flowers' fragrance wafted to me,
And the smell of the farm where life is so free.

HAYING

THEY are mowing to-day.
Yesterday the summer breeze tripped over the
      field
And the grasses bent slightly as it passed
And quivered in waves of silver eddies.
To-day there is the startling click of the ma-
      chine
As the great bay pair walk slowly about.
The grasses are falling like shattered hopes, and
The sun is beating down upon the wilting, warm
Clover and the ox-eyed daisies with drooping
Orange petals. Those daisies wilt so soon after
They are cut. There is a little girl, with dark
      eyes,
And brown curls clinging to her warm pink brow,
Picking up the flowers — poor wilting flowers:
The white daisies melt like snowdrops in spring,
And the poppies die like extinguished flames.
All the sweetness of the meadow
Is charmed forth by the sun, and the birds
Are singing sweetly as they flit over the field
Where the purple grass is falling.

HAYING

There is an agitated butterfly fluttering about
Like a lost soul — she is soaring over the field
And the dewdrops are her tears.
She is searching for something — she poises
And floats as the hawk after prey;
She is not hunting to kill, but there was a clover
She loved and it, too, has fallen.
She is restless, and her yellow wings flutter
Helplessly against the blue sky.
She stayed long on the perfumed plume of the
        clover
Last eve, and she cannot find it now.
She is stifled by the concentrated sweetness
Of the air so full of the breath of warm flowers.
There is a little gray mouse scudding like
A shadow over the leveled grass and flowers.
The mowing-machine does not stop
For the nest of a little brown field-mouse.
Under the shade of the walnut tree there is
A shiny pail filled with molasses and ginger.
I think that Ganymede never served to the gods
So pleasing a drink.
It has a piece of crystal ice in it,
And all the flower-sweetness mingles in that
        pail;

HAYING

That is why it never tastes the same
Anywhere but in the hay-field. It is so
Golden brown and so cool.
The sun is slowly sinking behind the hills,
And it sends out a golden glow
Over the field. The men are still at work
Just raking the last bits and stacking
It in cocks — oh, the sweetest, lightest cocks
To jump in and bury one's self in,
And listen to the crackle and struggle
Of a surprised cricket, and smell the mingled
Fragrance of every field-grass and flower
Warmed by the delicious summer sun.
Oh, there is nothing just like the hay-field.

TREE–FELLING

On a lonely far-off hillside
Where great pine trees grow,
Where the clouds hang low in summer
And warm breezes blow;
Where the dryads and the wood-nymphs
Dance beneath the silver moon
Till the stars come down to meet them
And the night is all in tune —
On the lonely far-off hillside
Rippled by a silver brook,
And the moss was green and lovely —
Many a trout-pool, many a nook
Where the fairies and the dryads,
Gliding from the hearts of trees,
Gazed upon a mirror surface
Till it vanished in the breeze.
To the lonely far-off hilltop,
To the fairy-haunted fell,
Came a chopper bringing axes;
Echoes answered through the dell,
And the breeze so warm in summer
Shrieked and moaned until the wood

TREE–FELLING

Answered in a low, deep thunder
All the fairies understood.
All the dryads in their tree-trunks
Trembled till their anguish swayed
The great pine trees on the hillside
And a deeper moaning made.
Click! the axe cuts deep and cruel,
And the chopper stops to see
That a fitful snow is falling,
Turns and chops more steadily.
Strange! he thinks the snow is falling,
He will never, never know
That the dryad of his pine tree
Has a spirit like the snow;
He will never hear her moaning
To the tree that held her long,
If he does hear he will tell you
'T is the echo of his song.

SELLING THE LOT

"Y'ER home at last and I'm glad yer be,
I ben waitin' fer ye to come see
The cow that was sick, she's worse to-night
A-bellerin' away in an awful plight.
Ye'd better go out and see her now,
'Cause we can't afford to lose that cow.
The summer folks 'll be coming along
And the cows and the hens jest can't go wrong.
I'll get yer supper while yer out,
And there's something else I'll tell yer about.
Farmer Stiles was over to-day
And told me the news 'fore he went away,
But come, yer must be after that cow
I can't stop gossiping it seems, anyhow."

She went with him to the little door
And gazed a moment or so before
Turning to cook the griddle cake,
And take out the pie she'd left to bake.
The cattle breath and the smell of hay
Mingled with the odors of waning day;

SELLING THE LOT

A stillness threaded the evening air
And the breeze ruffled her straight gray hair.

A hen with a brood of little chicks
Cackled and clucked between her picks;
The apple tree by the gate to the road
Blew in the breeze till its petals snowed
And the ground beneath was pink and white
Like hoar frost in the fall twilight.
The spring with the old pump, mossy green
And verdant grass that oozed between,
Stood there in the evening sun
Like a traveler when his journey 's done.
She stood in the doorway and gazed at this:
It always brought her happiness,
It always left the shell of a dream
And the vision of things she'd never seen.

She turned and vanished in the gloom
Of the little farmhouse, took her broom,
Swept the floor, and set aright
The kitchen table for their supper that night.
Then he came in — "Too bad," he said,
"But that 'cow 's beyond me, she 's lying
   dead;

SELLING THE LOT

And we ain't got all the milk we need —
Them summer folks is hard to feed.
I'll go to town in a day to two
And see if there's anything there I can do.
Did you say Jim Stiles was over to-day?
How is he and what'd he have to say?"

A flicker of pain flashed in her eye
As she cleared her throat to make reply:
"Well, Silas," she said, "Jim told me as how
He and the new man had an awful row
Over that strip of land, you know,
Between us and Jeremiah Snow.
It belonged to Jim and that rich new man
He's trying to buy all the land he can.
I guess he'll be askin' this next thing.
Would yer sell it, Silas? it looks good this
        spring."

Silas was silent a moment or two.
"I'll sell that land the last thing I do,
And never to him as long as I live,
And I'll make the will so's never to give
Him a chance to get it; look what he's did!
I wish to heavens the place was rid

SELLING THE LOT

Of him and his likes a-buying land
And struttin' around feelin' so grand.
Now 't aint that I 'm nasty,
But he shan't have this lot
He tells them around here, this house's a blot, —
Wall, I guess we 'd best be turnin' in,
Yer gettin' tired and a-lookin' thin.
It 's a long time since yer 've left this spot
Yer gettin' stale as like as not."

Through the weird candle shadows they stole to
       bed;
She lay awake, and thought how he 'd said
She was gettin' stale — would they ever go
Away from the place — she did not know
Whether or not she wanted to,
But she dreamed of things she never knew.
To-morrow would be the very same
As the day before — yet they say life 's a game.

THE TELEPHONE

I AIN'T lonely now like I used to be;
It 's funny how little 'll interest me.
I uster sit there day after day
And never a soul 'd pass my way,
'Cept onct a month the old mail-man
He allus brings me what news he can;
But 't aint so much — now I ken get
Morn'n a day than I used ter forget.
You see we 've put in a telephone,
Since they run the wires by Jim Malone's
Wall; the other day I heerd the bell
An I run to it — say, yer never heerd tell
Sech talk as it was. Yer know Jim Lake
And that gal with red hair, I see him take
Her to the dance in Jake's barn last night.
He called her to-day. Guess he likes her
        all right
"Hello," sez he, "how be yer to-day?"
She did n't seem ter hev much ter say.
"All right," sez she, "an' how are you?"
"Oh, I 'm feelin' fine — I allus do."

THE TELEPHONE

"How's yer mother, is her cold gone yet?"
"Yes, it's most all well, now if she don't get
  No more,—Say, are yer comin' over to-night?
  I was thinkin' as how perhaps you might."
"I guess not — I ain't milked the cow,
  An' it 's pretty muddy, anyhow."
"Oh, no, come on, it ain't so bad —
  I wish 't yer would, mar 'd be awful glad."
"Say, why don't yer talk louder, I can't hear;
  Yer not asleep, are yer, yer voice ain't clear —
  Well, I guess someone else is listening too."
I was just goin' to say as how I knew
Better and thet there wa'n't no one,
When I thought as how it would n't 'a' done.
I hung up all shakin', s'pose they knew
That I 'd been a-listenin' to them too!
But anyhow I hev a lot of fun,
An' most allus they don't suspect no one;
An' I hears more news than I heerd before —
There 's the bell now — I must run and hear
        some more.

THE SWAMP

THE spring grass grows green first in the swamp;
The elves of the brown earth
Chip slivers from a huge brilliant emerald
And thrust them up through the oozy black
     swamp mud
And the sunshine makes them warm and soft.
It is thrilling to wander through a swamp in
     spring;
There are many odors of the growing things
And the sunshine is always deep gold in the
     swamp;
The cowslips catch the sunbeams as they steal
     up through the earth,
And smile them back into the slimy water.
There is a wonderful glisten on the petals of
     cowslips
And their green leaves are fresh and shiny
And smooth for the fairies to dance on.
There is a beautiful mist that steals over the
     swamp at night,
And in the morning it is all gathered,
And lost in the swamp violets.

THE SWAMP

And the violet fragrance is the love-of-the-mist.
The huge veined leaves of the skunk cabbage
Sway in the breeze and seem always to try to hide
The purple and yellow hood beneath.
It has such an ugly smell when you pick it
And bring it into the house;
But its odor mingles with all the spring sweetness
And it just smells swampy out of doors,
And everyone loves the odors of the swamp.
The fuzzy curled fronds are fast growing
Into the beautiful lacy fan of the summer fern,
And they smell spicy and sweet.
It is always spring-time cool in the swamp
In the summer when the riot of flowers come
And flash their brilliant colors.
Still it is deliciously cool,
And fire-flies, the souls of flowers, glint in
Deepening shadows and thread the swamp mists.
They are gathering dewdrops from the air;
In the morning they melt back into the flowers
        again.
Almost every flower has a golden chalice;
The ones that have not are soulless
And the swamps do not love flowers without
Fire-fly souls.

RED–WINGED BLACKBIRD

Up from the swampy meadow
Where the tiger-lilies grow,
And the scarlet cardinal flowers
On their slender green stems blow,
Where the silver brook is calling
And rippling to the breeze,
Spot of black and flash of crimson
Flitting from the swamp-fed trees,
Did you touch that wing a-flying
On a maple's blossom red?
For the same clear spot of color
Flashes as you float o'erhead;
As you flutter bending earthward
On the jet-black shiny wing,
Orange-red as maple blossoms
In the freshness of the spring.

CHILDREN AND FAIRIES

FAIRY OF THE LEOPARD LILY

FAIRY of the leopard lily,
Dancing on a moonlit sea,
With an orange-spotted petal
Draped in splendor over thee.

All about the bells are ringing,
Dainty bluebells silver sweet.
Don't you hear a soft, soft rustle,
Fairy wings and fairy feet?

Fairy of the leopard lily,
Gliding in a moonbeam shell,
With a sea-sprite pink as sun mists,
Spirit of the wildrose dell.

See, a golden star is falling
From the singing summer sky,
Bright within the shell of moonbeams,
Glinting, darting fire-fly.

All about the moon-mist waters
Like a star that threads the blue

FAIRY OF THE LEOPARD LILY

Glide the fairies in the sea shell
Drawn by fire-flies of gold dew.

In the morning, by the sea shore,
Where the moonbeam shaft was drawn,
Someone found a scalloped sea-shell
Pink as are the skies at dawn.

And the flaming leopard lily
Swayed in anguish on the hill,
For the spirit of his wild rose
Stayed within the conch shell still.

SUNLIGHT FAIRIES

OVER the sunlit river,
To the heart of the silent hills,
The fairies of light are dancing
Like golden daffodils.

They gleam on the silver water
And smile to the sea-shell sky;
They sway in the evening stillness
Like love-thoughts drifting by.

They blaze all gold on the treetops
In a living, shimmering light,
Till the evening shadows deepen
That beckon the mystic night.

Then into the heart of the massive hills
They glide like a river of gold,
Until the petals of morning
In jonquil light unfold.

STAR REFLECTIONS

OUT of the mist of evening
Into the twilight sea,
The fairies from dreamland come fluttering
In a film of mystery;
And the diamond dew is falling
On all the sleepy flowers,
Velvet petals gently drooping
With the music of the hours.
The stars in the drowsy silence
Shimmer and fade and glow;
They love to die in the water,
A star reflection below.
And the little water-fairies,
Who dance with ripples that sway,
Take them and hold them for hours
Till bloometh the rose of day.
Then they kiss each star and it floateth
Up through the morning mist,
Into the life of the dawning sky
And the film of amethyst.

FOXGLOVE

Last night red fox was naughty,
He made faces at the moon,
And called the baby foxes
To the council rock too soon.
He scared the chickens on the roost
And woke the wise old owl;
He nosed a woodland fairy,
And he made an elf-man howl.

To-night the fairy of the glen
Chased him far and wide;
Red fox was very frightened
But he did n't know where to hide.
He ran about the forest,
And the dryads joined the chase;
The elf-sprites were delighted
And laughed at his disgrace.

But poor red fox kept running
Till he was tired out;
Then he crawled beneath the garden gate
And stopped to look about.

FOXGLOVE

But there the fairies caught him
And held him, oh, so tight,
Until they found a flower
By the moon's bright light.

They put one on each naughty paw,
Which made it hard to run —
A fox with gloves! The fairies
Thought that was the greatest fun!
Then poor red fox got up and walked
As good as he could be;
And ever since the flower
Has had that name, you see:
Foxglove with its pretty spots;
And so I 've understood
That fairies put it on the hands
Of those who are not good.

FAIRY SNOWBALLS

THE fairies had a snowball fight:
They made the balls of the moon all night,
They threw them about in the purple sky,
And laughed as they watched them gliding by
But soon they wearied of this wild game;
With children and fairies it's just the same;
And they left the silver balls lying there,
Moon-balls all glinting and gleaming fair.
Some people call them stars, you know,
But the fairies will tell you it is not so;
And if you watch some moon-strange night,
You may see a fairy snowball fight.

THE SLEEP FAIRIES

FROM out the valley of the moon
With its pale, transparent light,
Fairies come floating like soaring gulls,
And dance on the hills of night.

The fairy of sleep, with her drowsy eyes
And beautiful star-jeweled hair,
Wanders all dream-flower-laden,
And the fragrance fills the night air.

And all the fairies from sleep-land
In rainbow mists gently pass,
Leaving an empty dream-shell,
The diamond dew on the grass.

And the white moth fairy's flitting
Before the shimmering moon;
The frog and the cricket are singing
And trying to get in tune.

Just as the sky is blushing
With a thrill for the love of the day,
Thousands and thousands of fairies
Float in white mists away.

THE ECHO FAIRY

THE echo fairy's been busy to-day
.Over the hills and far away:
He caught the wind by his streaming hair
And held him till he filled the air
With moanings loud and angry shrieks
That echoed afar to the mountain peaks.
Then the echo fairy went over the sea
And caught its murmur of mystery.
Then back he flew on the breath of the breeze
And gave the sea-sound to the swaying trees.
Then he flew to the land where the daylight
      dies
And gathered the petals of fading skies.
He stole a dewdrop and flew afar
Till it echoed in the morning star.
The echo fairy has lots to do
Just echoing laughs of girls like you.
He tells me he likes that best of all,
 And he bears them away to the waters that
     fall.

RAINBOWS

I FOUND a rainbow, mother,
From the icicle light in the hall,
And I watched the rainbow fairies
Dancing upon the wall.

I found a rainbow, mother,
In the diamond spray on the lawn;
I watched the beautiful colors float —
But now they are all gone.

Do the fairies paint the rainbows
While they dance in the colors that lie
In an arch that touches heaven
And sees the earth whirl by?

Do they watch from the bridge of colors,
And faint in a misty haze?
Perhaps they all come gliding back
On the gold of the sun's warm rays.

A STAR WEDDING

THE stars were all a-tremble last night,
They twinkled and shone with golden light.
'T was especially thrilling up in the skies,
Where angels dream and the sleep-fairy flies.
You see a bright star was going to wed,
And she was very lovely, 't is said.
Of course, the moon would be there, too,
Because the groom was a moonbeam true.
A circle of light played round the star,
At least that's the way it looked from afar;
But 't was really the moonbeam crowning her
With the light of his life — the other stars
        were
All thrilling in gold through the purple sky
As the star and her moonbeam glided by.
On through the velvet night they sped;
They were coming to earth because they were
        wed,
And there they could live and love and gleam
Till the skies called them back on the breath
        of a dream.

A STAR WEDDING

We saw them in their earthward flight,
A glorious stream of living light;
And many thought 't was a comet, but we
Knew 't was the star and her moonbeam set
    free.

THE ANGELS' PATH

MOONLIGHT over a sleeping world
And a misty veil of dreams,
Studded with golden starry light
And woven of soft moonbeams.

Moonlight over a silent sea
And a hazy swaying light,
A quivering, changing path of gold
For the angels of the night.

HIDE-AND-SEEK WITH THE STARS

THE daisies last night played hide-and-seek
With the stars, and they promised not to peek
Till the little star fairies were hid in the sky
And the angel of morning was passing by.
One poor little daisy shut her petals tight,
But she heard all the stars hiding through the
   night.
How could she help but take one peep,
And then she said, "I'll go to sleep."
She opened her petals soft as could be,
Then she looked about, and what did she
   see?
Only one little golden star
That was n't yet hid in the morning far.
But the angel of dawn, who saw her peek,
Laid a dewy hand upon her cheek.
The daisy cried, for well she knew
That to peek was a naughty thing to do.
All day she was sad while the other flowers
Trembled and thrilled through the sunlit hours,
Waiting for the dusky eve to play
Hide-and-seek with the stars so gay

HIDE–AND–SEEK WITH THE STARS

And tried to find where the night before
They'd hidden themselves. But the poor,
Sad little daisy could n't play,
'Cause she peeked, and that's not a daisy's
   way.

THE SMELLING–SALTS AT THE DANCE

WE sat there each day and every night,
Forever on a plain cloth of white,
And we talked to the brush and the nail-file too,
But we longed for something more to do.

Sometimes her delicate fingers would touch
One of us, and we thrilled so much;
But you see we were only her smelling-salts
And even we have our grievous faults.

My lady was pink and I was blue,
And we loved as bottles all must do.
It was hard to wait for the silver light
Of the swaying moonbeams to come each night.

You see it was then we had our fun
And the bureau frolic was begun.
One night, when all were snug in bed,
We had a dance, and powder-box led.

The comb and brush were gliding about
And all the cologne came leaking out.

THE SMELLING–SALTS AT THE DANCE

You see the cologne bottle lost his head
Over a mirror-lady he longed to wed.

And we, my lass of pink and I,
Danced till we thought our odor would die.
Next morning the lady awoke to see
The bureau most disorderly.

'T was rather mean, yet we could n't tell
When all the blame on her, poor maid, fell.
We were all most terribly sleepy next day;
The powder-puff fainted and fell away.

The button-hook dropped to the floor with a bang,
And told the shoe that it could "go hang."
It's terrible after a dance, you know,
We're all so stiff, but we all love it so!

LOST

I LOST my temper yesterday,
And thought, What shall I do?
I hate to go without my temper —
Tell me, would n't you?

I looked behind the kitchen stove
And underneath the chair,
But still I could n't find my temper,
No, not anywhere.

Then I looked behind the bathtub,
Where the brightest sunlight shone,
And I saw a fairy smiling
At what she was sitting on.

An ugly black shadow
That tried to get away;
But I knew it was my temper
And I said, No, not to-day.

So I slipped it in my pocket,
But I took the fairy too;
Because the fairy of a smile
Can keep your temper for you.

A LONELY ALLIGATOR

FAR from the silver water,
Far from the wooded strand,
They brought him, a crawling reptile,
To a strange and far-off land.

Far from the tropic breezes
That fan the dizzy air,
They brought him, ugly reptile,
With dreams of his home so fair.

They brought him to his prison —
No golden glinting sand,
No palm trees to whisper to him,
No sun in this foreign land.

And he dreamed all night of the tropics,
Till a moonbeam gliding by
Paused a trembling moment
And heard a longing sigh.

Then she brought a dream before him,
Of a sunlit glittering sea,

A LONELY ALLIGATOR

And a mate that was calling, calling
From under a great palm tree.

And he crawled away to meet her,
And called the love-call back;
What mattered the prison to-morrow
After the joy of that!

CHILDHOOD

I THINK long, long ago, before I learned to walk,
I used to hear the fairies and woodland elfins
    talk.
I seem just to remember a fairy bright and gay
Who played with me and laughed with me all
    the livelong day.
I wish she would come back again, the fairy of a
    smile,
And play with me till I forgot my sadness all the
    while.
There were fairies in the flowers and fairies in
    the trees,
There were fairies in the whisper of every evening
    breeze.
Dear fairies, come again to-night and play within
    my heart:
The echo of thy voices make childhood visions
    start.

A SAIL ON THE MOON

DID you ever hear of the fairy
Who rides on the shining moon —
A merry-go-round, with the little stars
All playing their wondrous tune?
I saw him one night when the moonbeams
Had not reached down from the sky
To take their little fairy
Up to the moon on high.
He sat on a soft brown mushroom
Under the sighing trees;
He whispered and laughed with pleasure,
And teased the evening breeze.
At last the moonbeam came streaming
Through the branches and lay
In quivering golden silence
To take the fairy away.
I stepped on the beautiful moonbeam
While it lay trembling there,
And, do you believe me, dearest?
It bore me upon the air
Into the purple shades of night
To the shining orb of the moon,

A SAIL ON THE MOON

And I heard the little golden star
Playing a wondrous tune.
And then the moon began to sail —
O, dearest, try it some day:
Step on a golden moonbeam
And let it bear you away.

SUNBEAM

WHERE is the golden sunbeam
That came to your room to-day?
Did the elf of cloudland come, dear,
And carry it far away?

Ah no, I see it peeping
From out a baby curl;
That beautiful shining sunbeam
Is part of my little girl.

Should the elf of cloudland come, dear,
To take the sun from your hair,
Just smile, and the little sunbeam
Will hide in your dimples there.

FAIRIES

Fairies, when the moon is high
And the stars are passing by,
Fairies of the silver sea,
Dancing, dancing merrily.

Fairies, when the morn is pale
And the lily's waking frail,
Fairies on the shimmering sea,
Dancing, dancing happily.

Fairies, when the sun is up
Poising on a flower's cup,
Fairies on the golden sea,
Dancing, dancing merrily.

Fairies, fluttering near the rose,
Smiling while her petals close,
Fairies on a sunset sea,
Dancing, dancing happily.

MORNING MISTS

FAIRIES with your wings a-quiver
Underneath the pale moonlight
You have gayly danced and frolicked
With the spirits of the night.
Purple silence overspreading
Drowns the voices of the sea,
Till they murmur gently, gently,
Echoing fairy revelry.
Far beyond the hazy hilltops
Rise bright fairies to the day;
Morning mists we often call them
As we watch them float away.

THE ECHO OF A LAUGH

AWAY, way up the mountain-side
A beautiful fairy queen
Reigns o'er the moonlight fairies,
Two bands called Shimmer and Sheen.
The shimmering fairies go threading
Their golden way in the sky,
Till they hear the sound of laughter
As they are flitting by.
They gather the ringing melody,
And before they are even seen,
Fly back and give the music
To the silvery band of sheen.
All night in the heart of the forest,
To the music of laughter gay,
The moonlight fairies of shimmer and sheen
While the hours away,
Until the last star-fairy
Smiles from the morning sky,
And the lovely silver sheen fairies
Take the echoes of laughter and fly
Back to the children who smile at dawn
And lay them on the bed.

THE ECHO OF A LAUGH

Some children say a sunbeam
Is playing about their head.
They never guess that the sheen fairies
Have brought the echo there,
To make the day seem happier
When it ripples in laughter fair.

THE LOST FAIRY AND THE
AUTUMN LEAF

A poor little starbeam fairy
Lost himself last night
Along the path of the autumn moon:
She dazzled him with her light.

Poor little starbeam fairy
Did n't know what to do;
So he played he was a sunbeam,
And no one ever knew.

But at eve, when the golden sunlight
Called his children home,
The poor little make-believe sunbeam
Was left on earth all alone.

At first he was terribly lonely,
And almost began to cry,
When he spied more make-believe sunbeams
Peeping at him close by.

And then began such a frolic
As you never saw before;

THE LOST FAIRY

The little starbeam fairy
Was n't sad any more.

He took an autumn leaf by the hand,
And danced all that beautiful night,
And the moon did n't dazzle his eyes again,
But she smiled on such star delight.

Next morning the starbeam fairy
Danced to the morning breeze;
A little girl saw, and said, laughing,
"Oh, look at those playful leaves!"

FOREST STREAM

WHERE the rippling stream is brightest
And the golden sun is lightest,
Where the shadows glide and play
In rhythmic ripples all the day,
Where the cadence of a song
Fairy-uttered all night long,
Echoes in amongst the leaves
Of the murmuring sighing trees;
Where the moss is cool and green,
Where the moonlight leaves its sheen,.
And the fairies of the night
Dance to ripples of starlight, —
Take me there and let me be
A fairy of forest mystery.

A THOUGHT

THROUGH the dark and sombre pine trees
Slipped a golden gleam of love;
Woodland fairies hovering near it
Dreamed a star fell from above.
And they fluttered in the pale light,
As our visions 'round a thought
Quiver in translucent mystery
Till reality is caught.

SNOW

I WISH I knew what became of the snow
After the winter is gone.
Is it lost in the first white snowdrop
When the warm sunlight has shone?

No, I see it there in the heavens
That used to be cold and gray;
Clouds heaped so white and snow-like,
And they drift o'er the fields where snow lay.

They will fall again next winter,
Those beautiful clouds of white,
And lie sparkling in the sunshine
With diamond stars of light.

WHO CALLS THE FLOWERS?

MOTHER, who let the snowdrop out
From under the cold, dark ground?
And where did the crocus come from,
This one that you just found?

I think a fairy came to them,
And with her wand of light
Wakened the pretty flowers
From their sleep of winter night.

Do you think it was a fairy, dear,
Who brought the flowers of spring?
Who talks to the birds at evening
Until they gently sing?

No, dear, it is God's angel
Who kissed away the snow,
And called the little flowers
To see the sun and grow.

THE FAST LITTLE CLOCK

'T WAS the prettiest clock you ever saw
When it smiled its charming half-past four;
And it ticked and ticked with alluring tone
In the brightest way you have ever known.

The great hall clock frowned in despair
At the dainty clock with the piquant air.
There was one fault that she really had,
And grandfather clock thought her very bad.

She was fast; yes, alas, we must admit,
And besides she did n't care one bit.
She tossed her delicate hands 'fore her face,
And chimed with glee at the very wrong place.

A moonbeam fell in love with her,
But grandfather clock would ever demur,
Saying, clocks that are fast must never wed
But be punished very severely instead.

One night the moonbeam trembled near
To the fast little clock he loved so dear,

THE FAST LITTLE CLOCK

And said: "The stars in the sky'll not be
Aghast that you're fast, in the least degree."

So she went with him on the moon's gold light
And her lovely chiming was heard all night.
The fast little clock's as glad as can be,
Yet the jeweler said she was broken, you see.

THE TRAGEDY OF THE UMBRELLA

THERE was a green vase in the hall
Just behind the door,
Where all the canes were left, you know,
Instead of on the floor.
The tennis rackets stayed there too
All through the summer days;
But they were elite and went somewhere
For the winter months always.
But there was one umbrella there,
A lady of high degree,
She wore green silk and her handle was
As shiny as could be.
The hickory cane with the golden head
Loved her, and every night
The two would stroll about the house
In the spell of the deep midnight.
They were really going to be married,
And the hall-clock smiled with glee,
For he was going to marry the cane,
To the umbrella of high degree.
One summer's eve, e'er the nuptial day
Was set, the door-bell rang;

THE TRAGEDY OF THE UMBRELLA

The canes and umbrellas thrilled with delight
For 't was then their fun began.
They never knew just who would come,
And they always loved to see;
Perhaps Sir Golf Club or Base-ball Bat
Or le Français parapluie.
To-day, oh, thrills! who should there come
To the green vase in the hall,
And smile on the canes that languished there,
But the lovely Miss Parasol.
She was so dainty, all pink and white,
With her beautiful ivory head,
The gold-headed cane was entranced by her,
He forgot he was going to wed.
The clock in the hall frowned half-past four
And spoke to the frivolous cane;
The green umbrella wept as though
She 'd just come in from the rain.
At last Miss Parasol sweetly smiled
And ruffled a lacy good-bye;
We never knew what became of that cane,
Miss Parasol and I.

THE LAMENT OF A FEATHER

WHAT a sad ending!
Packed so tight we cannot hear
Our shrill-throated chanticleer,
Cannot see the sun's first light
That used to wake him after night —
What a bother! Here we are
Packed like sardines in a jar:
I, who used to glint and shine
In the sun, now peak and pine
In a pillow. Oh, I hate it!
Yes, I knew my life was fated;
For the coxcomb told me so;
He's the soothsayer you must know,
And he said my life would be
Very dark, and you can see
That every word he said was true.
I tickled my hen, all feathers do
If ever they get excited, and then
We ruffle a laugh at the funny old hen.
But dear me, those good days are o'er,
I don't tickle hens or laugh any more

THE LAMENT OF A FEATHER

In this stuffy pillow — Never mind, some day
I'll scramble out and get away.
My sister did it, but sad to tell
A worse fate was hers — she fell
Into a dust-pan all shiny and black;
Just as she thought she liked shellac,
A hurricane blew her with bristly ire
Into the hungry flames of the fire.
Oh, my poor sister! I heard her cry,
As she flew up the chimney, a feath'ry good-bye.

IF I WERE A RED, RED CHERRY

If I were a red, red cherry
Away up in a tree,
With lovely, shiny skin
And warm sunbeams on me,
I think the thing I'd like the best
Would be to touch the sky —
It comes so near to cherry trees.
And, of course, I'd grow up high
Where little boys can't reach, you know,
And where the butterflies
Please to flutter — Oh I would
Just love to touch the skies,
And feel the softness of the clouds
In banks of snowy white;
I'd love to stay and touch the moon
When it comes out at night.
If I could touch the soft blue sky,
I would never be afraid
Of the robins and the crows because
They do not dare, it's said,
Eat a cherry if it can but
Reach the soft blue sky.
Perhaps I'll be a cherry some day
And have a chance to try.

I CANNOT UNDERSTAND

PAPA is very polite, you know,
And Mama says I must be
Just like him — take off my hat
When a lady speaks to me,
And always stand when older folks
Come in, and tell them all
How glad I am to see them.
And 't was nice of them to call.

Papa is very polite you know:
He carries things for Mama.
Of course, it does n't make much
      difference
Just how heavy they are.
The other day Papa and I
Were walking home together;
The rain was falling and the wind
Just made it awful weather,
There was an old woman walking
With a big bundle in her hand.
Why did n't my Papa help her?
I cannot understand.

THE LOST THOUGHT

FAR away in the land of the stars
Where the golden moonbeams play,
And the starlight fairies hide at night
When they hear the whisper of day;

Far away from the hands of life,
Over the sea of dreams,
A beautiful love-thought went astray
And was lost in star-land gleams.

Long it wandered among the stars
And played with the moonbeams light,
Till one tender, beautiful moonbeam
Brought it to thee in the night.

MOTHER'S FLOWERS

I HAVE a lovely little garden with lots of pretty
flowers;
And they like the nice warm sunshine and they
love the gentle showers.
It's fun to see their tiny eyes shining, oh, so
bright,
When it's been raining ever so hard all through
the night.
Mother has some pretty flowers, roses and
pansies too,
On a little cloth for the table — it's just about
sky-blue;
But those poor flowers nearly died because the
rain can't fall
On them and make their eyes shine bright, and
the sun can't come at all,
So I took a pitcher yesterday and gave them
water to drink;
I don't see why God forgot them and mother
was angry, I think.

DREAM–CHILDREN

Just a bubble; it touched the earth there, see!
Just a dream and it touched reality.

By the fireside, in the golden flames,
Two children are sitting playing games.
Soft flaxen curls about her head
And his dark brown just tinged with red.
Oh, see the soap-bubble floats in the air;
The colors are so lovely — rainbow fair;
And how they love to watch it! Mother dear,
'T will touch you and be broken; look, it 's near!

I think it touched; there 's nothing now to see,
But a drop of water where the bubble should be.

MOTHER-LOVE

THE last ember died in the fire-grate;
With it her life-light was extinguished;
And she left this for her baby child —
Perhaps it was because it was all she had,
Perhaps she had a reason which God knew.
It was a mirror — a little piece of forest brook
Where there were no ripples, where it was smooth.

The child gazed sadly into the mirror;
She saw her mother's face — she was crying:
"O Manda, mother is sad and it is raining;
I am sad too — I am sad like the evening breeze."
Manda looked into the mirror;
She kissed the child and the child smiled.
"Look again in the mirror," Manda said.
"Oh, mother is happy now, her face is smiling."
"Yes," said Manda, "mothers are happy when
Their beloved children are."

FANS, FANCIES AND FRIVOLITIES

WHY?

WHY do your eyes say one thing and your lips
        another?
I hear you speaking of the lightest things in life,
Things for a child to say, and laughing as a child.
I hear you laugh and see excitement take you
By the hand — whisper something in your ear,
And you speak of life's most sacred things in
A mocking ridiculous jest.
And I look into your eyes, beyond the outer blue
To thy inner self, thy silent thoughtful self that
        I love,
And your eyes do not say what your lips are
        saying.
Why do your eyes say one thing and your lips
        another?
Why does your mind stay back like a frightened
        deer
In the thicket, while you utter thoughtless vani-
        ties?
Your truthful eyes tell me that you love
A sacred thing — sacred of all things, and,
Being so, the easiest to revile. It were useless

WHY?

To say more. I see your eyes say they
Are longing for something, — peace, quiet,
A sunny field and a grass-banked brook
Where cowslips grow and honey-suckle scents
      the air.
Your lips say you are delighted here,
Odors of perfume stolen from the fields.
Words do not paint the contrast as vividly as I
      know
It is painted in your own heart. Still I
Must wonder why your eyes say one thing
And your lips another.

HER NEW FAN

SHE took me with her last night to the ball;
I was her most favored trinket of all;
For she held me in her hands, you see,
And often whispered and laughed through me.
At dinner I lay on the cloth of white
And blinked in the dazzling shining light.
I've never heard such a noise in my life;
I did n't dare speak even to the knife
That lay beside me and smiled with glee
For he was used to such gayety.
My lady was laughing, and talking too
About such funny things perhaps she knew;
But I, being only a feathery fan,
Don't understand all some people can.
At ten by the grandfather clock in the hall
We started off for the country-club ball.
"Hello, Louise, I just love your dress,"
My lady smiled in prettiness;
"Oh would you please see if my powder shows —
I had to put such a lot on my nose.
I love your hair, will you show me how
You do it some day? I love the bow —

HER NEW FAN

Oh come, let's go now. Where's my fan?
Can you keep yours? I never can."
That hurt my feelings a bit, you know,
And I felt my feathers softly blow.
Then we went upstairs and she laughed some more
With the men who were standing at the door.
More glaring lights and a strange loud sound;
I ruffled my feathers and looked around.
She said, "Have you seen Louise to-night?
Her dress is ugly, a perfect fright.
I don't see how her mother can
Let her wear it — and oh, her fan!
But come, I'm dying to dance, are n't you?
Oh, look! There's Sally, she's dressed in blue,
And the way she's done her hair is new."
To repeat all I heard in the next few hours
Is beyond me and all my fan-like powers;
But if you want to know, read this again,
For all she said seemed just the same.
At last, when morning was almost here,
My lady and I came home, — I fear
A little the worse for wear.
She sat by the mirror and looked at her hair.
Perhaps the mirror could tell you best
Just what she thought and all the rest.

HER NEW FAN

She put me away with her old, old fan,
And we talked together as only fans can,
While I told of all that had happened that night
Under the glaring electric light.
The old fan spoke in a voice soft and low:
"My child, it was just so years ago."
To-morrow we'll talk to the minuet fan
And see if 't was the same since her life began.

A QUESTION

WHY do you like her? I should love to know.
She is very pretty, I grant you that,
And your favorite flower's the one on her hat;
And she is a girl and very sweet —
The kind of a girl all men like to meet,
With golden hair either curly or curled
And teeth very pretty, white and pearled;
Her eyes are lovely, most all girls' are,
And they do have brightness like a star,
Especially if they like you; but oh,
I forgot, it's why you like her I want to know.

Well, that's hard to explain, if you analyze,
Love must always take us by surprise.
I don't know just why — you say she's a girl.
And she's very pretty with hair a-curl
And tender eyes that laugh into mine;
I like to watch them when they shine.
I don't really love her, not yet anyway,
I might, you know, yes, I might some day.
She is different from me, but that's the best way —
Something you know, like the night and day;

A QUESTION

And I like in her what's lacking in me —
Laughter and fun and frivolity.
It's such a good change from my prosy life
Of everyday work and toil and strife;
And she has brains, not the brains of a man,
But a bright, quick mind that understands
All the delicate lightness of life,
And that, too's a change from my strain and
     strife,
But there's no one reason that I like her, you
     see —
Just she's a pretty girl and attractive to me.

THE MIRROR OF A FICKLE GIRL

SHE bought a new hat yesterday,
With roses pink and a bow of gray.
It was very pretty — she thought so, too;
Girls always will when a hat is new.
The minute it came, in its striped box,
She put it on her soft brown locks,
And the tissue paper blew to the floor —
The mirror smiled — "How many more
Hats, I wonder, am I going to see,
And reflect each 'as pretty as can be ' ?"
How much the shiny mirrors could tell
If we listened, for they know too well,
Not only what we are wont to say,
But they know all our thoughts — gay
And sad. She put on the hat and smiled to see
How pretty she looked — "Will he like it on me?"
The mirror heard her whisper, and thought,
"I wonder for whom this hat was bought."
Had ever a mirror so much to do
In reflecting and remembering who
Had to be pleased by each new hat!
Oh, we mirrors are always doing that.

HIDE AND SEEK

I CANNOT find you;
I have hunted, but in vain.
I must call you forth
Or else you will have to speak and tell me
Where you are.

I cannot find your real self;
I have searched and thought I found it;
But I know it is not your real self now:
This tinsel clink of flattery, these light words,
They are not uttered by your real self.
Is it that you have very cleverly hid yourself,
        and do not want
Me to find you? I have searched long.
Will you not speak one true word from your
        heart
And let me know where your real, lovely self is?

Others have told and the game is ended.
There is no searching after we have found.

THE ROSE ON HER HAT TO THE
ROSE ON THE BUSH

SAID the rose on her hat
To the rose on the bush,
"Good morning, and how is the sun?
I've stayed so long in the closet dark
That I did n't know spring had begun.
That's a beautiful butterfly hovering near —
They never will come to me.
I wish I were growing just like you:
How wonderful it would be!
I never can feel the breath of spring
Or long for the blue of the sky,
And try and match it to the shade
Of the blue bird fluttering by.
It must be so lovely to feel the dew
On the velvet of your leaves,
And whisper back to the murmur
Of the spring in the dreaming trees!"

Said the rose on the bush
To the rose on the hat,
"I am tired already of spring,

THE ROSE ON HER HAT

And the butterfly seems so far away.
Oh, what can the dewdrops bring?
For I must fade and droop in the sun
Warm, wilting petals of pink."

I wonder which is the happier rose?
Tell me, which do you think?

THE STRAY LOCK

IT was a lock of curly hair:
The wind kissed it and thought it fair.
Dancing a ringlet dance it went
With the playful breeze in soft content.
It laughed, and a sunbeam gliding down
Mingled its gold with the lovely brown;
A little hand gently pushed it back,
But the bad, stray lock did n't mind that.
It was sick of staying with the rest —
The wind and the sunshine were much the
        best.
Besides there was such a dimply smile,
'T was fun to see it once in a while.
No, I don't blame that lock of hair
For loving the sun and the breezy air.

And least of all — for I 've strayed, too,
To see that dimpling smile — Would n't you?

A LETTER

A LOVE-DREAM sheathed in paper-white
Passion the lurid leaping light,
And it burns for a moment red and clear,
Then vanishes, taking all that was dear.

SCANDAL

Who started the snow-ball of rumor
Rolling down life's hill
In precipitous flight
That loses sight
Of the summit of truth until
It lies besmeared with scandal?
When it melts and leaves
What the world believes.

A PILL

A GLASS of water
Pure as the sunshine on the sea,
Clear as the air that sweeps the lea —
And a pill.

A small white pill, —
An unpoetical thing, you say;
And yet, pray cast it not away.
Think on it.

This pill in water —
Is it not thus that our thoughts dissolve,
In the billows of life as the years evolve
And are lost?

You'd call them lost?
But they flavor the substance in which
          they melt
And grant me their essence still is felt,
Like the melted pill.

ALONE WITH FANCY

Just to be alone, and think under the blue sky;
Just to be alone, and see day-dreams floating by;
Sunlight over the water, mermaids over the
   sea,—
Alone with sound of breezes and life's wonderful
   mystery.

Just to be alone, and listen to the lisping of the
   breeze,
Trembling kiss near to the branches of the bud-
   promising trees;
Far beyond the lacy hilltops, dreams and dream-
   trees are floating by,
And my thoughts drift out to meet them, as they
   mingle with the sky.

Just to be alone and silent, midst the murmurs
   of this life;
Just to be alone, forgetting that there ever must
   be strife;
Till the shadows of the evening gently quiver
   over all,
I would sit and dream and answer to a far unknown call.

A FANCY

LIKE mist-clouds drifting o'er the lea
Her garments fell beside the sea,
And lay in white foam on the beach,
Wind-blown beyond the wavelets' reach;
Far in the shades of the evening sky
Sea-gulls, foam-born, floated by.
Still she stood like a swaying flow'r,
Silent in the twilight hour;
A Goddess 'gainst the murmuring sea
Wrought so pure and fragilely.
The quivering waves reached out to touch
The limbs they'd borne and loved so much,
And a beautiful fluted sea-shell lay
On the sand like rosebuds cast away.

THE BIRTH OF VENUS

A sunset shell beside the sea,
Soft flushed with rose-breathed mystery;
A rainbow spray that lay in foam
On the beach of her Ionian home.

And all about the faintest mist,
Like a dream of hazy amethyst;
Far o'er the sea of silent light
Breathed rosebud skies to greet the night.

And primrose shadows were mingled too,
Fading in the deep sea-blue;
A sea-sprite gathered all the light
And laid it in a shell this night.

Smiled o'er it and she was born,
Venus of light and love, next morn,
With rose-breathed limbs and hair of gold,
Eyes of sea-blue and depths untold.

They found the pink shell on the strand,
Clasped in the glistening silver sand,
And a rainbow spray that fell in foam,
On the beach of her Ionian home.

A FANCY

'T WAS morn!
I looked and saw a face bending over mine;
I heard a voice — the voice that lilies have lost;
I raised my lips to meet thy fragrant lips,
And then a mist fell over me and my world.

'T was noon!
I thought warm waves of sunlight fell on me,
But when I looked it was thy wonderful hair;
Oh, it was like the ripples of eternity;
And then a mist fell over me and my world.

'T was eve!
Something in the murmur of the far, far sea,
Something unuttered wafted to my ears;
I looked into the heaven of thy eyes, to see
No mist, but thou in living, trembling glory.

'T was night!
And a deep dreamy peace was in my heart.
With the voice of the velvet-footed star-beams
You called me, and my soul leaped apart;
It took you, not I, and held you in throbbing love.

GARDENS AND FLOWERS

HER GARDEN — MY GARDEN

WITH the perfumed breath of each flower
Mingling in the breeze;
With a jasmine mist over the waters
And a whisper of far-away trees;
The primrose sky faint smiling,
Touching the lips of night —
Her garden — my garden, I love you
In the mist of waning light.

In the paleness of moon-lit shadows
Swaying to and fro,
Where the heliotrope breathes to the silence
And slender hollyhocks grow;
Where the fairies dream-winged
Are rising out of the dewy grass —
Her garden, my garden, I love you
In the soft star-gleams that pass.

Fresh morning with floods of sunshine
Pouring over the hill;
Diamond dew on the flowers,
And petals that tremble and thrill;

HER GARDEN — MY GARDEN

Pink to the morning sunrise
The moon-kissed hollyhocks sway —
Her garden, my garden, I love you
'Neath the fleecy clouds of day.

LILY OF THE VALLEY

Lily of the valley, with your pretty bells,
Can you keep a secret that the spring breeze
      tells,
Of the golden sunshine and the rainbow dew,
Of the flower fragrance wafting forth anew?

Lily of the valley, with your bells so white,
Can you keep a secret of the summer night,
Of the glorious sunshine, of the fragrant flowers
Breathing into silence of the silver hours?

Lily of the valley, from every opening bell
Wafts a springtime secret you thought not to
      tell;
All the fragrance of the breeze, the mystery of
      each star,
The beauty of a summer night breathes forth
      near and far.

THE LOTUS

Lily of mystery and charm,
Lily of ecstasy and harm,
Lily of sleep and long forgetting,
Consciousness is but a fretting.

Beautiful lily of visions and dreams,
Thy petals are faded and all life seems
But a lingering tear in a soul of delight, —
Beautiful lotus of lavender light.

CANTERBURY BELLS

PINK bells, purple bells, bells of purest white;
Ring them, dainty fairies, all the mystic night;
Chiming on the waters to the silver moon,
Chiming, chiming, chiming, all the night's in
      tune.

Pink bells, purple bells, bells of purest white;
Ring them, pretty fairies, till the dawn is bright;
Till the echoes flying far beyond the hills
Wake the drooping lilies and the daffodils.

Pink bells, purple bells, bells of purest white;
Ring them, little fairies, in the gold sunlight;
Till the daisies answer and the heart shall hear
Fairy bells a-ringing, chiming sweet and clear.

Pink bells, purple bells, bells of purest white;
Ring them, airy fairies, when eve dims the sight;
Chime them to the sunset and the rising moon;
Sweet the air with bells a-chiming in the fairy
      tune.

WHITE LILY

WHITE lily atilt on the waters,
Smiling gold to the sky,
Dreaming of clouds and soaring birds
And breezes wafting by.

White lily afloat on the waters,
Sweet as the joy of a dream,
Watching the mystic moonbeams
Shimmer and glint and gleam.

Lily afloat on the waters,
Folding thy petals of white,
Life of thy life enfolding,
Thou art lost in the love of the night.

Lily afloat on the waters,
Lovely thy petals of white;
Faint are the golden heart-throbs;
Thou art lost in the love of the night.

A GARDEN

THE golden sunbeams linger
On the dew of the velvet grass,
And the long, long shadows of evening
Silently, softly pass.
The heart, too, is wont to linger
Like the sunbeams here, you know;
For 't is such a lovely garden
And the flowers are fair that grow,
And the long, long shadows of sorrow
Melt in the moon's soft light,
In this dream-garden made of beauty
And love and spirit-light.

HELIOTROPE

LACY flowers like the mist
Of evening distant amethyst,
Breathing perfume to the skies;
Charming, passing butterflies,
Yellow wings that fluttered far
To rest on perfumed lavender;
Emerald flashes dart and float
Humming-birds with ruby throat,
Jewels flashing one by one,
Diamond dewdrops in the sun —
Lovely, fragrant heliotrope,
Emblem of undying hope,
By the moonbeams softly kissed
Dreaming dreams of amethyst.

WHERE LILIES GROW

BLACK as the shadows of the night,
Black with a streak of bloody light,
Across the smouldering evening sky
The flames of fire have serpented by.

The trees are naked every one,
Like a gnarled and twisted skeleton.
Like a thought of consuming pain it swept,
Like a viper it hissed and hungrily leapt.

And here we stand on a wasted plain,
Bespeaking horror, blackness and pain.
This one little pool escaped the fire.
And from the oozy night-black mire,

One lily as pure as the upper air,
A water-lily, is floating there.
White petals out of a black despair
Gold stamens into the sullied air.

There was a city as black as the wood,
Charred with despair and devoid of good;

WHERE LILIES GROW

The blinding sheet of fire and pain
Had swept it and left it blacker again.

Out of the sin and mire of life,
Out from the killing rancorous strife,
Another lily lifted her head
Out from the rabble of morally dead.

And she was as pure as the lily that came
Where the greedy fire had leapt in flame.
In this life of mystery lilies of snow
In sin-black mire and waste may grow.

FORGOTTEN

The butterfly promised the rosebud
To come to her at dawn;
He forgot and the rosebud withered
With the drooping mists of the morn.

And the little butterfly fluttered
Over the summer fields,
And sipped of the gorgeous poppy
And the nectar that clover yields.

At eve with wings a-tremble
The butterfly came again
To the rose, but she had vanished;
How many have known her pain!

I KNOW

DEAR ROSE, thou wast but a bud last night,
Only a dream-tinged promise of the flow'r
Before me now, this rainbow sunlit hour.
Tell me, dear, of thy most rare delight.

Dear girl, but yesterday I saw thee young and
      fair;
What of the new light in thy maiden eyes,
Deep as the mystery of summer skies?
Yesterday only a mystic promise was there.

Dear rose, hath love come unto thee as well
And charmed thy delicate petals apart;
Mirrored all life in the depths of thy heart?
Dear rose, I will not ask that thou shouldst tell.
I know.

A VIOLET

ALL in a violet —
The freshness of the dewy spring,
The echoes of the birds that sing,
The flutter of a downy wing, —
All in a violet.

All in a violet —
The rays of the warm and golden sun,
The pureness of a day begun,
The shadows of the evening done, —
All in a violet.

All in a violet —
The loving thoughts that fill the air
And breathe their sweetness everywhere
To make the dream of spring more fair, —
All in a violet.

All in a violet —
The tender love I bear for thee;
All that thy life means to me,
With a faint, far dream of eternity, —
All in a violet.

A PATH

THERE was a woodland path — you know
The kind, where Indian pipe-stems grow
Because they love the darkest place,
To stand in ghostlike fragile grace.
Silently and lonely I wandered through
The deep, black wood where the pine trees
      grew;
And all of a sudden a shaft of light
Pierced the depths and shone there bright,
Dazzling in its beauty rare;
And the grass was green and flowers were fair.

THE BROOK

WHAT is the little brook saying,
Chattering all the day,
To the leaves and grass and flowers
That bend on its waters at play?

I think it sings of the great fields
That the wood-flowers never see,
And the warm blue sky and sunlight, —
The brook is so wild and free.

It sings of all the flowers
That make the air so sweet
With the perfume of dainty petals,
When the wind is playing fleet.

And it sings of love and laughter
And yearning longing, too;
I think perhaps it guesses then
That I am longing for you.

TANSY AND CHICORY

A SUNBEAM fell to earth and shattered lay
Among the swaying shadows of the day.
Then evening smiled, a magic sunset smile,
And night of mystic dreams came the while.

Next morning in a field, gold tansy grew,
And here and there a touch of heaven's blue;
You've seen such spots full often, so you know
How fair it is to see a sunbeam grow.

CRIMSON ROSES

CRIMSON roses in the garden
Breathing to the pallid moon;
Velvet petals soft and fragrant
Warmed by sunbeams gold at noon.

She so loved to walk among you,
Crimson roses, warm and sweet;
And you held the silver hours
Of her life that slipped so fleet.

Slipped like glimmering mists of morning
Out into the great unknown;
Gently, gently palpitating,
By the wind of death-sleep blown.

Crimson roses in the garden
Filling all the moon-beamed night,
Are the angels singing to you
Of her spirit pure and bright?

SONGS AND SEASONS

SONG.

Oh, the music of the sky
When the stars are passing by,
And the angels up on high
Breathe a song when mortals sigh.

Oh, the beauty of the night
When the moon its splendor bright
Sheds in rainbow shafts of light
On the fairies of delight.

Oh, the wonder of the day
When the last star melts away,
And the birds with voices gay
Sing a joyful roundelay.

Oh, the peace of evening when
The daylight breathes amen,
And the mist o'er vale and glen
Charms the day to night again.

And the music of the sky
When the stars are passing by,
And the angel songs on high
Echo soft when mortals die.

YOU

Her robe was the dusk of the evening,
Her hair shone with silver starlight,
Her eyes were filled with the haze of a dream
That spreads its strange way through the
      night.

Her cheek was the blush of dawn skies
When the morning star fades from view;
Her soul was the spirit that fills the air,
And her beautiful self was you.

SONG

TAKE me over the hills, dear,
Far, far away;
Take me into the distance
Beyond the light of day.

Into the far, soft shadows
Where the daffodil star's agleam;
Where we can love, my dearest,
Love and live and dream.

Take me into your life, dear,
As the night enfolds a star;
Take me into your arms, love;
The world is pleasing afar.

Oh, just for a perfect moment,
Bury my pain in thy kiss;
The pulse of life is throbbing
In this transcendent moment of bliss.

A SONG

Out of the mists that lie over the lake
The fireflies glint and the wood nymphs
       awake;
Out of the primrose evening sky
Fragrance of flowers is wafting by;
The silence is bringing a dream to thee
From rainbow dell of mystery.
Far, far over the lofty hills
Sleep the wanderer stops, and fills
Her iridescent goblet with light
And strange misty fragrances rise through
      the night.
The star of evening far, far away
Is glimmering of what the angels say.

HER HEART

Pale as transparent moonlight
That waxeth gold with the dawn,
Fair as the spring-fresh morning
When roses and violets are born.

Her heart, as an evening primrose
When the shadows of pain o'erspread,
Opens in tender beauty
To smile at the night overhead.

A MYSTERY

Strange life and stranger love!
Who can understand
How much pain and joy is fate —
How much hath God planned.

Strange life and stranger death!
And then — the still to be;
Fate is in the hand of God
And all is a mystery.

SAILING

I WENT for a beautiful sail last night,
All through the star-lit sky;
And the swaying glinting moonbeams
Silently shimmered by.
The clouds were soft and dreamy
And they rocked the boat to and fro,
As the pine boughs rock in rhythm
When the gentle breezes blow.
And I sailed through the golden silence,
Where the angels float in mist,
My boat, the shell of a lovely dream,
Floated in amethyst.

SPRING AND FALL

SPRING

IT is spring:
There is a beautiful restless sadness in the air;
So much that is lovely,
And we are so small to enjoy all
That makes the soul restless.

Lovely spring:
It has taken my soul away somewhere —
To a cloud, I think, —
But it has left me here
With the exquisite sense
That I am part of this luxuriant dreamy spring.

I hear a voice calling.
Who is it that calls?
It sounds as the evening sounds
When it calls out the gold-tipped stars.
I love to hear it.
Now it is like the voice of the red-lipped poppy
Calling serenely sweet to the bees in the fields.

SPRING

Spring is so deliciously feminine!
It tells secrets as maidens do;
It has the faint indecision of a girl
And all the luxury of promise;
And the stars on spring nights
Are maiden-eyed.
There is a sweet convincingness about the spring,
A clinging tenderness;
And the nights are full of love.
There is so much behind the moon on spring
        nights!
The angels touch a tender chord in spring;
That is why the breeze is so soft.
It would be a sacrilege to be boisterous
In the dreamy silent silence of a spring night.

SPRING ECSTACY

Oh, wild and joyous ecstasy,
Tinged with the joy of expectancy,
How perfect and complete!
I think the world is made of light,
With purple stains of rich delight,
Of love and harmony.
Soul, thou hast reached the height of bliss;
What can be more sublime than this!
My heart be still.
This is the height of dewy spring,
When the trees bloom and the birds sing
In merry roundelays.
The heart answers in throbs of delight
To a voice that is calling out of sight,
The voice of exultant spring.

SPRING PROMISE

SHE was so like a dream of springtime,
With its freshness and misty shades;
Her eyes were like the lovely moonbeams,
With a wistful shadow that fades.
The flowers had breathed on her tresses
And the sunlight had sought them there,
And loved to stay, for it found them
Exquisitely dainty and fair,
Like the petal mists of morning
When the rose sunrise shimmers through;
A mystery hovered about her,
A promise that might come true.
Dear little soul of the springtime,
In whose world wilt thou fulfil
The beautiful promise of love and life
That God hath granted us still.

A BIRD'S CALL

THE call of one bird,
And over the hills a stirring,
Is heard, as though the spirit of spring
Were trying each misty fluttering wing.

The call of one bird,
And out of the ice-freed silver lake
The mists of morning rise and shake
Rainbow dew over hill and brake.

The song of one bird,
And in the far, faint echo I hear
Thy voice, I see a vision appear
Of thee in thy loveliness drawing near.

The song of one bird;
The breezes are answ'ring o'er the sea —
Thou and the spring come back to be,
Each a part of life's mystery.

All in the call of a bird.

THE SPRING MOON

THE crescent moon rose over the lea
Out of the rippling shadows of the sky,
Where dreams and visions floated gull-like by,
And lay upon the bosom of the sea.

Beneath the waters of aqua marine
A conch-shell lay, pink-tinted and curled
Like petals of the rose unfurled,
Deep in the wonder of the ocean's green.

The crescent moon sank into the sea
Deep to the heart of the curved conch-shell;
The primrose petals of morning fell,
And the conch-shell lay on the lea.

An echo of waves on the shore of sleep
Deep in the heart of a shell on the strand,
And a glitter of gold on the silver sand,
The crescent moon that sank into the deep.

A SPRING SONG

WHAT makes the spring air so soft?
Is it the thoughts of love,
Or the dreams we have dreamed
That vanish into the blue sky above?
Is it the whispering flowers.
Or the breath of the silvery moon,
Or is all the spring air sweetness
Just that the heart is in tune?

BLUE SKY OVERHEAD

THE soul in me is not yet dead
Because the blue sky overhead,
The springtime sounds that fill the air,
Thrill me still and seem so fair.

To-day I saw a little bird,
And his sweet caroling overheard;
My heart thrilled like an evening breeze
And trembled like the white birch leaves.

This eve the air is springtime cool,
Sweet as the freshest summer pool,
And all the world is full of spring,
Full of dainty imagining.

THE BLUEBIRD'S SONG

LITTLE bluebird of the spring,
Tell me, in the song you sing
Of the flowers and the trees,
To the rippling of the breeze,
To the skies of thy own hue —
Little springtime bird of blue.

Yes, I sing of trees and flowers
Through the lovely summer hours,
To the breath of soft blue skies,
To the water's fall and rise,
To the sunshine and the dew,
And, little girl, I sing to you.

FALL FLAMES

I WATCHED the greedy flames of fire
Exultant, leaping high and higher,
Wild and lawless, ruddy, bright,
Full of lurid passion light.

It burned an hour like life afire,
Thrilling and rising ever higher;
Then the glow died in its own wild flame —
Died like the vanishing dream of fame.

An ember fire smouldered low,
Tenderly warm like breezes that blow.
It did not die in its own wild light,
But glowed with warmth through the long,
      fall night.

FALL SKY

THAT is my life,
That gray sky with a gash of red,
The one bright spot of a hope that is dead:
You've seen such skies,
And you've loved most the gash of light.
So do I love all my life that's bright —
I love it best.

A LEAF — A LOVE

A CHEERLESS sky:
The wind is high,
And the leaves are gone from the tree.
One trembling trace
Of summer grace
Is left for the world to see.

A golden leaf
To the winds of grief,
But the dream of summer is there.
We gaze at it,
And bit by bit
Forget the winter despair.

Two souls that part:
A broken heart
And dead hopes drift on the wind.
Love gently clings
When life's other things
Are lost to the grief-sick mind.

A LEAF — A LOVE

In love we see
Life's imagery,
The dream of the purest and best.
The leaf on the tree,
The love that shall be,
Endure all and stand the test.

CHANGE

How all things change! Last night the summer
    breeze
Trembled and quivered through the leafy trees;
This morning there are murmurs far away,
Long, lazy shadows like the ocean sway
Across the sunlit grass. I cannot understand:
The selfsame scene I saw last night, the strand
That smiled unto the summer sun;
But, oh, how changed! The honied fall has come;
The air is clear as fairy bells and thrills
The throbbing heart, but, oh, deep down fills
It with drowsy, aching pain;
The fall of waning life hath come again.

A DREAM OF THE FALL

PALE yellow leaves of autumn
Like warm shadows of the sun;
Petals gently falling
From the flowers one by one.

Long, long evening shadows
Steal across the lea;
Flaming sunsets flash their color
On the stormy wind-tossed sea.

Honey in the scented air,
And katydids that call
Shrilly in the quiet night,
And we dream the dream of fall.

AUTUMN CONTRADICTIONS

QUIET, golden autumn days
When the heart is in a maze;
Exultant 'neath the mellow sun,
Regretful of the summer done.

Quiet, lustrous autumn nights
Ablaze with heaven's fiery lights:
The splendor of the harvest moon
Creates a ghostlike, earthy noon.

Quiet, weeping autumn hours;
A day of contradicting powers;
Flaming leaves that soon pass by;
A love within a heart to die.

RELIGIOSA

IN THE NIGHT

In the long, long, silent hours,
In the velvet folds of night,
Hours that cry out to the darkness
And faint within the pale starlight:
When the sad heart aches and trembles,
Crushed beneath the palm of pain,
Soft a voice comes from the silence,
"Bear thy cross; 't is not in vain."

In the long, long, silent hours,
Wild with soul-consuming grief,
Throbs the heart in bitter yearning,
Groping, longing for relief.
Soul, be patient; in the darkness
Thou canst neither see nor hear,
But a hand is reaching tow'rd thee —
Christ, the sufferer, bending near.

RESIGNATION

SHE is at rest —
That thought doth fill the heart
And quell the bitter tears that fain would start:
She is at rest with God.

She is at rest —
And for her sake we bear the aching pain
Until our hands perchance shall meet again,
In God's great peace.

She is at rest —
Peace, peace, my soul, her spirit is too near,
That this unthinking grief should form a tear:
Hers is the perfect peace.

GOD KNOWS

THERE are times when the heart is o'erflowing
With the bitter elixir of pain,
When the clouds hang low in heaven
And the mist is changed into rain.

There are times when the tears from the heart's
       depths
Well up in the longing eyes,
Bleed through white lids that tremble,
And the butterfly hope-dream dies.

God knows these hours of our suffering,
And His angels bend yet more near:
I think sometimes that heaven itself
Is reflected in a pure tear.

MELROSE ABBEY

HERE in the time-dimmed ages of the past,
Hearing sweet chimes upon the morning air,
Shepherds and good town folk might repair
To kneel in unmolested peace, and cast
The burden of their sins away at last
In the deep, voiceless sea of faithful prayer.
The spirit of those souls must still be there.
We enter. The great window, stained and glassed
So long ago, now frames the green fields, and hills
Beyond. The chimes' reiteration fills
The air, the dainty bluebells rung
By fairy hands, while distant hymns are sung
By angel choirs bending o'er us here.
What wonder that we hold this spot so dear!

WHERE NOW STANDS TRINITY

WHEN the golden moon is high,
Gliding through the silver sky;
When the night is cool and damp
As with vapors from a swamp,
Where the mists are slowly falling,
Where the whippoorwill is calling,
And the swamp grass, fresh and cool,
Grows within the black mud pool;
Here before me I can see
A church, men call it Trinity;
It is but a shadow now
Hid among the leafy boughs;
Birch trees bending in the breeze
With their palpitating leaves,
Flowers breathing in the air
Perfumed jasmine-sweet and fair.
From the white mists o'er the lake
Glinting fireflies awake,
Starring all the mist swamp dell
Till the Indians of the fell
Wakened by their shimmering light
Come and dance all through the night.

WHERE NOW STANDS TRINITY

Here a path leads to a pond
And a bright light shines beyond, —
Mystic, glittering path where play
Water-nymphs with the waves that sway
Where the water-lilies float,
Like a dream-shell fairy boat.
Through the water slowly wading,
From the faint mists gently fading,
Comes the deer with timid eyes
Out of the forest's mysteries,
Stands a moment in the shadows
Scenting the far-distant meadows,
With the dew-damp wilting flowers,
Sleeping through the silent hours.
Soft the dream is fading, fading,
And the fallow deer is wading
To a faint, far-distant shore
And I see her now no more.
Here, where long ago she fed,
On her mossy flower-strewn bed,
Where the crickets all a-singing
Chirped — ah, list! a bell is ringing,
And the Christian church is here
Where was once the haunts of deer, ,

WHERE NOW STANDS TRINITY

And the moon that saw the dell
Hears the ringing of the bell —
Knows what years have brought from out
Love and heresy and doubt:
It is strange how oft I see
No church, but a dell of mystery.

THE GOLDEN CROSS

Lost in the vast cathedral of the night
My spirit wanders on dream-wings of prayer,
And revels in the sacred wonders there;
The purple pillars and the shrine starlight
That trembles with angelic breath, then bright
As palpitating moonbeams, but more fair,
Burns to consecrate the holy air.
Reality is far beyond the sight,
A dizzy sphere where worry, pain, and loss
Are held by faith in a golden cross.
And God is on His throne in the skies,
Smiling on joy and on life's tragedies,
Gazing, yet not sorrowing. He knows
That bearing pain and suffering, the soul grows.

SOLACE

I THOUGHT an angel came to me last
And stood before me in the misty-visʌ
Her voice was soft as moonshine on the sea
And all its splendor melted over me.

Thine was the voice, my dearest, from the night,
Thine was the vision and the perfect light;
My Mother, thou art ever near to me
Since God hath set thy perfect spirit free.

SHADOWS OF GOLD

How long the shadows linger on the grass,
Waiting, perhaps, for her they loved to pass.
Soft shadows, I have waited, too, in vain
To see her — oh, to see her once again.

Gold, sunlit shadows, now you move and sway,
I see a vision, too, beyond the day;
Far in the shades of evening's rose-soft light;
Shadows of gold, she is with us to-night.

SONNET

STILL there? Or is it but a dream of two
Who long ago kneeled in reverent prayer
Here by the arm of this fireside chair
While night of star-eyes and mystery drew
Near and laid her hand gently as angels do
Upon them? What of a world of dim despair!
Only the tender spirit of prayer was there;
O God, how swift those blessèd moments flew!
The hands of night must now spread far to reach
The aching spirits and to comfort each;
And yet before the dear old chair it seems
They two in prayer, hand clasped in hand,
Still linger. Life is hard to understand —
Reality resolves itself in dreams.

IN MEMORIAM

Now is the cycle of a year complete,
With all the changing light and shade of chance,
And all the balancing of circumstance.
Ah, me, the white-winged days are fleet!

AN ANGEL

SILENT I sit here in the dead of night;
Far off the wondrous mystery of starlight
Repeats itself in sparks of trembling gold,
A baby lamb bleats in the distant fold;
All else is still, and perfect peace prevails
Beneath the pow'r of the Love that never fails.
Sacred and holy is the very air we breathe
Gently do the unexpressèd thoughts wreathe
Themselves around a fresh and quivering wound.

A voice from out the silence, sweet and low,
Mingling with the gentle winds that blow
A face; move not, my heart, it is her own —
The same dear blessèd face that thou hast known
And loved so long. To-morrow thou wilt say,
"I saw an angel in the night that flew away."

CRUCIFIXION

We stand once more before His cross to-day,
Thou and I, living those three long hours again,
The hours of suffering and untold pain.
The shadows of the evening steal away
And leave a twilight of repose, to stay
The throbbing thought. He died for us, what
      gain,
O thou, dear one, was it all — all in vain?
We do confess Him, we have learned to pray,
And yet our hearts can see Him suffer still,
Cleave to our own desires, forget His will,
Add one more thorn to that death-plaited crown,
And watch the life-blood flowing slowly down.
Oh, could we but resist such sin that He
Might be rejoiced that moment in some slight
      degree.

A PRAYER

God keep thee, dear,
Through all the wondrous starlit night;
Through all its mystery of light,
God keep thee, dearest one.

God guard thee, dear,
While all the light and shade of chance
Sways o'er the field of circumstance;
God guard thee, dearest one.

God bless thee, dear, thy life and mine,
And sanctify our sacred love,
Make it more pure and more divine;
God bless thee, dearest one.

PORTRAYALS

A PORTRAIT

She is lovely, see her dainty head
Profiled against the sunset golden-red.
There is a classic beauty in her face,
Madonna-like, exquisite in its grace.
Titian dreamed the lily of her arms
And rounded neck of maiden charms;
A mist-gold sun of long ago
Is all around her — Oh, you know
The way Correggio might have seen
Her ringlet hair with its golden sheen;
And she is here, an echo of that art,
Perfect and lovely with a woman's heart.

A GIRL

Do you hear a laugh
And then look to see
Who the merry soul may be?

She laughed and I looked about at her
And met two shining eyes;
She was not lovely or even clean —
Tell me, is that a surprise?

Did you think she was really going to be
A beautiful girl with golden hair,
And warm, pink cheeks that softly blushed
And red lips alluringly fair?

She was n't, and if you like only that kind
Don't read any more or you will be
Utterly disgusted. She was sitting on the
        common bench —
You know the kind, where you see

A GIRL

Every creature that God ever planned,
And when the warm springtime comes
Lovers sit and coo like doves
Sandwiched between the worst town bums.

She had a lover — and called him her beau —
And she sat there like the rest
Chewing gum and pulling it out,
And, mildly to say, she was gaudily dressed.

With white shoes — once clean, perhaps,
But they certainly were n't that day —
And a skirt that rivaled the poppy,
Because it was so gay.

And a hat with a frail pink feather;
If it saw the skirt, it looked white
And it dropped with very shame, because
It simply could not look bright.

Her laugh was just like the dress she wore,
Loud and gay and bright;
And her brown eyes twinkled merrily
With a mischievous, pretty light.

A GIRL

And her fingers, with rings that children find
In prize candy boxes, you know,
Fiddled with strings and stretched her gum
As far out as it would go,

And she held the other end in her teeth:
She may have been ugly,
But she had the whitest teeth in the world
And they glistened like pearls from the sea.

Her hair was straight as the string of her gum
And it blew all over her face;
I think she had some gypsy blood
Or belonged to the Indian race.

I've seen many girls and I've loved a few,
The pretty ones pink and white,
But I envy the lad that sat on the bench
With the little gum girl that night.

She was n't clean — her hands were grimed —
And she was n't pretty at all,
You might n't like her, but I did,
And what are mere looks after all?

THE TEAMSTER

THE heavy team rumbles along
And the teamster is singing a song,
Singing in mindless delight;
And his song when he's out of sight
Echoes upon the air,
Echoes in vague despair.

He has come to the end of the day —
One more — spent the selfsame way
As the one before, with the rattle of stones
As he jars along — it would break your bones
To ride there with him
And to hear the loud din.

It is just five minutes to five —
It will take him an hour to drive
With the heavy horses that walk so slow
Back to his home, and the white snow
Is just starting to fall.
He stands and he's very tall

THE TEAMSTER

Against the blue boards of the cart.
He wraps the horse blankets about him smart
And the horses are still shuffling on,
A motor car passes and is gone
In a flash — lost in its dust
They would not take it — but the teamster must.

The snowflakes are melting in his face;
The water trickles down to trace
The deep wrinkles about his chin;
His pipe smoke rises in a thin
Blue thread of smoke,
Acid enough to make you choke.

He is almost home now; in his eyes
If you thought to watch them the tragedies
Of life would vanish, giving place
To gentler lines in the rugged face.
The black door space has taken him in
To his home, away from the rattle and din.

THE MINER

HE blinks at the clear sunlight
With eyes that have seen black so long,
With eyes that no longer are strong
To greet the radiant day.

He has come out of the earth
Where it is blacker than night,
Where only a blinking lamplight
Flickers a gruesome smile.

The coal dust is as his face
Streaked white from the sweat of his brow,
And his weak eyes see better now
In the brilliant sunlight.

His muscles are strong as iron
And his hand is calloused and scarred;
Cramped from gripping the shovel so hard
Into a crumpled claw.

THE MINER

We cannot look at his heart
Under the ragged suit of clothes;
Under that heaving breast — who knows
What his thoughts may be.

Forged from the heart of the earth
Where only a few men can stay,
Those thoughts are different, they say,
From the thoughts of other men.

A ROMANCE OF THE CIRCUS

THE tent was close and smelly and hot;
The polar bears had the coolest spot,
But even their long, red tongues hung out
As they wagged their heads and swayed about.
The zebras dozed in the sultry air
And thought of the grass in Africa;
The baby giraffe was munching hay
And his mother was dreaming of the day
When she was caught in the noose of rope
And dragged down the wooded jungle slope.
The elephants stood over by the door
And their swaying trunks swept on the floor:
There were two more this year than there'd been
        last ––
Two more to dream of a jungle past.
The children laughed in wild delight:
It reminded the elephants of hyenas at night.
"Skinny," — one elephant turned his head, —
"Look at that little tot dressed in red,
The one with the flower on her hat,
Do you remember the girl who looked like that?

A ROMANCE OF THE CIRCUS

The same sort of sad gazing in her eye,
She allus looked like she was goin' to cry.
Do you remember her, Skinny, old man?"
Skinny swayed his trunk, like elephants can
And blew through his nose — "Don't believe I
    do."
He said, "Tell me about her, could n't you?"
"Well, 't was when you first came to join the
    show;
I'd come to it — oh, let's see — years ago,
But I've never forgot that girl or the clown
Who allus used to take her aroun'.
The clown was the tall one they called 'Old
    Skate,'
And he slid on my back and held my slate.
When I added two and two, which made four,
It delighted the crowd — they used to roar
With laughter and fun; then the girl's act came.
She was a trapeze girl, and one night she got
    lame;
She'd been practicing almost all the day
And Old Skate was there, he hung round that
    way
Wherever she was — well, this day she fell —
She could n't get her balance well,

A ROMANCE OF THE CIRCUS

And she hurt her foot; Old Skate watched it all.
He turned sort o' white when he saw her fall
And went to her and took off her shoe.
It was dirty and worn, and she had her blue
Dress with the short skirt that day.
Old Skate lifted her up and took her away,
He in his old white clown suit and she
All in blue, like a little fairy.
She could n't walk, and that night I heard
That they'd bounced her. Skate did n't say a
      word
To any of the folks exceptin' me;
'Con,' he sez, 'it's this way; you see
They won't have the little girl no more
And she's gone away — she went before
I could even tell her I'd like to go
And sort o' take care o' her, yer know.
I give her the money to get away,
But I reckon I'll go too — I can't stay
Now that she's left; there'll be another clown
To slide on yer back and bounce aroun'.
I'm goin' to-night, Con, and I'll find her too
She can't hardly walk, — whatever 'll she do?'
He sat there thinking far into the night
But he warn't there with the morning's light.

A ROMANCE OF THE CIRCUS

I thought of him for many a day.
Skinny, I guess that's the elephants' way.
They don't forget when they like a man.
Well, in three or four months the moving began;
Then the bustle of pitching the tents and all:
The circus life's like the waterfall
That rushed and roared in the jungle where
I come from — only 't was more peaceful there.
Well, first thing I heard when we got to town
From one of the horses that goes aroun'
And prances and dances through the street
To tell folks, 'This show can't be beat.'
'T was Old Bally told me, the best he could
Knowing well as how it would
Break my heart to hear he was dead.
It warn't no use their going off, he said;
At first they were happy as could be —
They lived together awhile and he
Cared for her and gave her some things
That belonged to his mother — some clothes and
       rings;
Valuable 'nuff, I guess, for she went
An' pawned one or two; but afore she spent
The money, he had her caught
An' all crying and sobbing they brought

A ROMANCE OF THE CIRCUS

Her to the judge's place and they made her go
To some sort o' prison — not a real one, you
      know,
But Old Skate was nearly crazy. He cried
An' raved about; said he wished he'd died
Afore this. A yeller cur heard him say
He was goin' to get the girl away.
He went to the prison-like where she stayed
And tried to tell them that he'd made
A mistake and to let her go,
But that's not the way with the law, you know.
So then Old Skate he broke his heart;
His face was all white and his lips hung apart.
He went next day to the prison again.
They would n't let him see her; so when
He could n't get in, he sent a word
To ask her to marry him. Then he heard
As how she'd said she never would;
So Old Skate he went away for good.
The yeller cur followed him all around;
He said he was in some dream and the sound
Of his sobbin' wuz pitiful to hear.
Well, he went home with all that wuz dear
To him in the world, gone. The yeller cur
Listened awhile and he thought of her

A ROMANCE OF THE CIRCUS

In the prison — Old Skate thought too;
Just to sit and think, 't was all he could do.
The next mornin' some folks came in and found
Old Skate lying stiff and cold on the ground.
He'd shot himself — Skinny, us folks of the zoo
Have a queerer life than most folks do.
There's the little tot again in the red
With the sad-lookin' eyes — Skinny, look ahead,
Is n't that her mother standin' near?
She's the trapeze girl, do you hear?"

The little one stretched out her hand to say,
Welcome—the mother turned and led her away.
And the two great creatures swayed to and fro,
Reaching out their trunks as far as they'd go.

REMINISCENCE

It was a musty old closet,
Filled with boxes and things,
With funny old bangles for dresses
And feathers for hat trimmings.
It is funny how they remind us
Of the clothes we used to wear;
We lived in them and now they tell us
The thoughts that have lingered there.
They remind us of what we were thinking
And whom we were loving then,
When we left them there in the closet.
If we should wear them again,
They never would seem so pretty
As we used to think they were,
And our thoughts would be foreign to them
Because we were so much older.
The dust was gray on the boxes,
And there was a musty smell,
But you must have rummaged through
        store-rooms
So you know the mêllée too well;

REMINISCENCE

How the dust streams to the window
Where the sun is struggling through,
It glints and gleams so prettily,
As the wings of bright fairies do.
I sat there opening boxes
And living over the days
That were far out on Time's horizon,
Dimmed by an ambient haze.
With listless, dust-stained fingers
I opened a long, thin box,
Thinking to find wrapped bundles
Of cloth for the children's frocks.
Oh, tell me, have you ever
Locked a love away
In the deepest spot of your heart's depths
And felt it again one day,
Stirring with untold longing
And yearning for what is past,
I opened the lid and found my doll
And I took her and held her fast.
I had loved that doll with the passion
Of the hungry heart of a child;
I had cried to her, sung to her, talked to her,
And she always sweetly smiled;
I had kissed her as mothers kiss children

REMINISCENCE

Till the paint all left her cheeks,
And her hair that had once been curly
Was matted in yellow streaks.
Her eyes had never changed, though,
They were just the same china blue,
But they used to say they loved me;
I think all dolls' eyes do.
I had put her little dress on,
And then hid her away,
Because the folks kept saying
I was too old to play
With dolls; that I ought to sew
And learn to sweep and cook.
She had that same dress on to-day
And the same sweet, smiling look.
Oh, all the love of another day
Flooded back on my heart,
And all the dreams of my childhood,
Till I felt the tear-drops start.
I kissed her dear, hard cheeks again,
As I kissed them long ago.
The angels of Doll Land had guarded her
All through those years, I know,
And the joys and sorrows of childhood
Flooded back again.

REMINISCENCE

The strange, little childish worries
That used to bring so much pain;
I heard a voice that I have not heard now
For many longing years,
The voice of the one who gave me the doll
And used to dry my tears;
I know not how long I sat there
Holding my darling doll,
While the dust streamed to the window
And the sunbeams danced on the wall.
I did not stay that morning
To find the cloth for the frocks.
I put all my dear, loved childhood
Back in the little doll box,
And I kissed the faded cheek again;
It was foreign among the rest.
I think the doll loved the kisses
Given in childhood best.

POSSESSION

HE sought her in the morning,
When the sun was shining bright,
With eyes of adoration
That languished for her sight.
And she was like the south wind,
Gentle, sweet, and free.
She loved, but, ah, thou seeker,
Her love was not for thee.

He sought her still at noontime,
When the golden sun was high,
And like the breeze of evening
She saw, but passed him by,
As oft the swaying shadow
Flees the ardent wind.
He loved her, longed to win her,
Vowed she should yet be kind.

He sought her still one evening,
She did not fly from him:
The wind was gently sighing
And the sunset growing dim.

POSSESSION

They heard a secret breathing
All through the sunset haze,
Stealing into their fond hearts
Until love was ablaze.

Like the slender lily she bent
Her graceful head,
"I love you, dear," and all the trees
Echoed what she said.
And then her loving heart depths
Yielded him love and bliss;
He sought her lips and reveled
In her pure maiden kiss.

The love weeks passed as flowers,
Wind flowers on the hill;
One morn he did not seek her,
He said, "She is mine still,
Why strive to hold what stands and waits,
I will not seek her more?"
Possession strangled what had been
Questing love before.

EONS AGO

SHE was a creature fair to see,
Wild and impulsive, ecstatic, free;
And this was eons and eons ago
When the world was not the world we know,
When the jungle sang to another moon
And the nights were all like the nights in June.
He was a creature tall and strong,
His shoulders were broad and his arms were long,
And the fleetest-footed deer that ran
Could not outpace this primal man.
And they wandered under the great palm trees
And waded in water up to their knees,
And for many a year they lived close by,
But she never came beneath his eye;
And he hunted the forest and killed the deer
And she lived on berries and fruits that grew
      near.
One morning under the flame-colored sun
They met and each feared the other one;
And he was strong and he thought to kill,
But an unseen power turned his will.

EONS AGO

And she fled through the forest, this fleet, wild
    thing;
He followed swift as a bird on the wing.
Over the ragged hills they sped
And ever the form of the woman led;
And her golden hair streamed in the wind;
He could almost reach it from behind.
And the morning sun smiled down in gold
(He has often smiled so since I am told),
But the warmth of the sun's smile wearied her.
Still he rushed on, ever getting nearer,
And he caught at the beautiful golden hair.
His arm was strong and he held her there,
And she turned as the doe turns when at bay,
And her eyes spoke what her lips should say.
She struggled in vain to be free once more.
He held her, but not as he held her before,
Not to kill. Have you seen a child hold a butter-
    fly
When it longs to be free and it fears to die?
She was still for a moment. He felt his heart stir.
Then eons ago as it is to this day, he spoke to her.
She could not understand, she tried to run again.
He was a man — and to the thing he loved gave
    pain,

EONS AGO

Roughly he grasped her wind-caressed throat dried
From the chase and clutched it till she cried.
Those crystal raindrops bleeding from her eyes
He had not seen before, and strange surprise   ,
Gripped his heart. What creature could this be,
What animal had stirred him thus strangely?
He did not know that love was in his heart;
He only felt a strange new throbbing start.
And the sinking sun saw tear-drops in his eyes.
The thing he loved fell to the ground and could
       not rise.
The purple marks of his great hands were there
Upon her neck so delicately fair.
Gently he lifted her and bore her to his cave,
This animal of all he hunted he would save;
In a silvered shell he brought her water then
From the bubbling stream in the rainbow glen.
She lay on the jagged rocks all limp and frail,
The cave was black and her limbs were pale,
Like moonbeams on a beauteous summer night,
And her hair streamed over her in golden light.
And the man stood in the door of his cave,
The man that was tall and strong and brave;
And this was eons and eons ago
In a strange, past world, but we who know

EONS AGO

Love, know the stirrings the primal man felt
As by her side he tenderly knelt
And gave her water to drink from the shell.
A moonbeam that strayed in the cave could tell
How she moved and opened her dizzy eyes
And gazed about her in rapt surprise;
How he lifted her gently in his arms,
The creature he caught, but then dared not
      harm.
And the moon was high o'er the silver lake,
And the dewdrops glistened upon the brake,
And the breeze was wandering through the wood,
Quietly as though it understood.
And the moonbeam that strayed into the cave
Saw the first kiss that man ever gave
To woman. And this was eons and eons ago.
The moon has cast its splendor here below
Many and many a night since then and seen
Many loves and wooings in its silver sheen,
And the moon will tell you, if you ask to-day,
That we too love in the primal way.
That the creatures who sped o'er vale, and hill
Are racing, pursuing, and loving still.

VERS LIBRE

TO ——

WHY do I think of you so often now?
I did not love you.
When we sat together under the white pine tree —
I did not love you then.
Why do I think now of the time you spoke to me
And smiled into my eyes?
I thought the sun was shining,
But it was the glory of your smile.
And I repeat in my heart what you said to me
And I love the words now.
They were only words then — now they are
       treasures.
The wind can never blow
The lovely gold heart of the daisy away,
Nor can time waft away the memories of that
      day,
And I am glad.

There will never be a day like that again:
The next time we meet I shall know that I love
      you
And it will all be different —
A beautiful, strange difference.

TO ——

I have a fear in my heart, and yet I know not
    why.
It is a silent fear,
But you will lay your hand on mine,
And I shall see your eyes gazing into mine
As summer skies contemplate still waters,
And then I shall not be afraid,
But shall only love —
Love you with all the strength of my soul —
And I will be exquisitely happy.

A FANCY

It was evening
And the purple spirit of the sky
Lighted the star lamps;
The moth flitted silently before the moon.
There was a long beach of glinting sand
And it shone in the beauteous light.
I sat on the border of the sea,
Like a soul on the edge of the land of dreams,
And loved. My heart throbbed in my breast
There on the moonlit sand, where the
Foam waves broke in passion on the shore.
I learned how to woo a woman
The way the waves wooed the beach
Under the moonlight.
The sea spoke in the voice God gave
The winds eons ago and took from them again.
The voice of the wind and waves is much the
      same.
My eyes reached out over the foamy, limitless sea
To a far bright spot,
And a great gold star came down
And lifted the figure of a woman from the sea,

A FANCY

Held her against the struggling sky
And kissed her with the passion
Of his soul, held her and
Kissed her again. Then he
Let her fall back into the sea
And her white arms were lost in the foam.
To-morrow I shall win thee, Love of my life.

PARTING

I DID not love to let thee go.
It was like going from home,
Going to some far-off land
That eyes have only glimpsed in dreams.
I do not love the foreign, lonely darkness
I feel when thou art far from me.
The evening had a sad, impressive beauty,
And it was a spring evening
When the flowers bloomed in fragrance
And the stars looked languorously down
And the breeze took thee away.
Something light stayed near — I felt it —
I think it was thy spirit.
How long will that stay? The moon
With snowy steps is coming out of the hill,
And there is a shadow under the cedar tree.
I have an exquisite aimlessness in my
Sleepy soul and only thy spirit is near me.

MAGNOLIA BLOSSOMS

THERE is a sleep flower blossoming in the garden,
And there is one blooming in my heart,
With exquisite cream-white petals that droop
    apart
In an adorable languorousness.
There is a spirit hovering over the magnolia
    flowers,
She is the spirit of dreams,
And her soft moon-white hands
Are pouring visions into the flowers.
When they fall, some one will dream a lovely
    dream
And the pink-tinted petals
Will bear away all that might grieve the heart.
There is nothing but love and happiness
In the sleep blossoms of the magnolia.

CLOUDS ACROSS THE MOON

THE souls of unbloomed roses are on the breeze;
There is a drowsy dream-substance in the eve-
  ning air;
Only the garden fountain pierces the silence
Like a silver lance of falling diamonds.
My soul is the echo of the aspiring fountain,
But my heart is asleep on the fragrant couch of
  eve.
I am glad my heart is sleeping, for thou art afar,
And it is anguish when thou art not here.
There is an exquisite sadness in the tops of the
  trees,
And the wind is shaking it out into the night;
And so the tops of the trees are swaying tremu-
  lously.
I see a shadow standing under the linden tree
Reaching white, fragrant arms to the lowest
  branches,
And singing to the thousand mysteries of the
  spirit-night.
She is singing the song God taught the valleys
  long ago,

CLOUDS ACROSS THE MOON

But they forgot it. It is the song of a passing
       soul.
Half the moon is behind the cloud to-night,
And there is a pale-blue light in the skies
That fringes the cloud. One of the angels loved
With mortal love to-day — that is what spreads
       a cloud
Across the mystery of the silvered moon.

MARRIAGE

THERE is a golden circlet about thy finger
And one about mine.
That is all the change the world may see in our
      lives.
I have a sacred fear within my heart,
So many of my dreams have come to earth
And broken as a rainbow bubble vanishes.
I feel thee near me now —
My lips have long sought thine in lotus dreams —
Now they may touch and sink into the fullness of
      a kiss,
As the gold-winged butterfly poises on a flower,
Then in sublime contentment
Sinks into the depths of its sun-warm chalice
And lies insensate there.
My longing hands do not touch darkness now,
Not darkness, but the sublime tenderness of
      thine own,
And only God in his greatness can know
Of the infinite vastness of my bliss.

MARRIAGE

The breeze is fanning the waning stars
In an adorable tenderness.
Thou and I alone in all the beauteous profun-
     dity.
Two clouds scudding the silent skies and meeting
     at last,
Two shadows blended now beneath the moon,
Yet the world sees but a golden circlet about thy
     finger
And one about mine.

POT AU FEU

THERE was a kitchen
With pots and pans that shone brightly in the
   sunshine,
And in the evenings the copper light of the fire
Made them glow flame red.
On winter evenings, when the snow was heaped
White and soft outside and the wind howled
Around the corners of the house,
The family gathered about the kitchen stove
And talked or read by the old lamplight
In the center of the table with a red cloth on it.
In its little drawer was the cook-book with recipe
   papers.
Those were cozy winter evenings and the
Simple talk of the peasant folk rose above
The simmerings of the *pot au feu.*
The *pot au feu* was upon the stove day in and
   day out,
Year after year, always simmering
And unconcernedly boiling.
The bubbles rose and broke
Like unrealized hopes dream-fed;

POT AU FEU

All the odors of the cooking mingled in it
And scraps from the dishes fell into its turmoil.
Long it boiled, the fire was carefully tended
So it did not boil over. Those were peaceful,
      happy days.
But there came a day when strange news
Reached the family.
Strange news that struck terror to the heart,
Gripped their lives and paralyzed their inten-
      tions.
Mothers neglected their homes and wept
Over a son or a father they were to see soon
Departing. Daughters wept over their sweet-
      hearts
Who would soon go from them. It was only
A rumor then that war had been declared.
The mother neglected the home heedlessly.
With mind awander, she heaped fuel on the fire
And left it to go to her room and weep
In unconsoled despair.
And when she came again to the kitchen she
      found
The simmering *pot au feu* had boiled over.
Clouds of putrid smoke filled her nostrils
And blinded her eyes. It nauseated her

POT AU FEU

And filled her with a dizzy faintness.
She flew to the window,
With trembling hands tore it open,
And little by little the smoke cleared.
The objects in the kitchen became visible —
The little table with the red cloth, the old oil
      lamp
And the red geranium on the window sill.
She went to the stove. The *pot au feu* was
      empty —
Only a reddish-brown clot that was
Almost blood clung to it; all else was black
Like strips of the dead of night, and the
Stove was reeking and filthy with the
Charred mass from the boiled-over pot.

It will be some time before the stove
Is returned to its former glory,
And the family will not soon gather about it again
Because of its putrid odor.
It means a good deal when the pot boils over.

Should you stop to ponder over this a moment
On the simmering *pot au feu*, on the boiling tur-
      moil of the *pot au feu*,

POT AU FEU

Of the charred black desolation and spoil of the
    stove,
Mayhap it would call to your mind something
    greater.
Nations simmer year in and year out and at last
    boil over,
Then God only knows the charred despair
That is left on the blackened field of war:
God only knows the months and years — cen-
    turies of struggle
To regain the lost glory of these nations;
And the families for many a year will not as-
    semble
In love and quiet under the shelter of a nation
    at peace.
The charred stove will not soon be clean,
But how much longer will it take for the horrible
Stench and stain of bestial war to be eradicated
    and obliterated?

A RHAPSODY

I HEARD the music of floating clouds,
And a butterfly that had not flitted the dew from
      her wings
Passed by. Sorrow lay like Pompeii, silent,
Under a mindless sky. Tragedy too was buried,
The red-lipped poppy swayed in tranquillity
And the clovers breathed in the air.
A bird rose from the purple grasses,
Scattering wing diamonds to the yellow sun.
It seemed strange to be in the world and
Yet far away from life. The moon came up,
And my heart turned, so did the
Flowers; in an exquisite languorousness
The moon passed through the temple of night,
And there was a voice that spoke
From out the hills — yet not the hills' voice —
I think it was the voice of God.

L'ENVOI

HEART SONGS

THE birds sing at morn
And their songs mingle in the sounds of the day:
The flowers breathe all their fragrance to the air
And it vanishes beyond the blue ridges of the
      hills.
The sea murmurs of its million mysteries,
And the echoes beat on foreign strands,
And life speaks to life.
The heart sings and its echoes rise
And flood the radiant, eager air.
There is but one thing that shall hush
The singing of the heart on this earth,
And after that it shall sing elsewhere, mayhap.

CPSIA information can be obtained at www.ICGtesting.com
Printed in the USA
LVOW03s1204030414

380168LV00005B/434/P